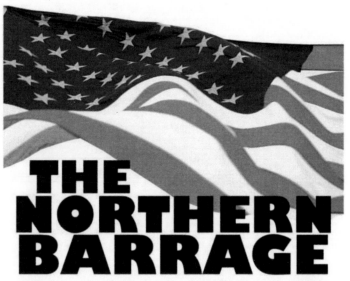

THE NORTHERN BARRAGE

The Fence Across the North Sea in WWI

"In 1918 an ambitious scheme for establishing a line of guarded minefields across the 180 miles of water between Norway and the Orkney Islands was developed by the British and American Navies. Enormous quantities of materials, regardless of cost or diversion of effort, were employed upon this supreme manifestation of defensive warfare."

Winston S Churchill
The World Crisis 1911-1918

A Mark VI mine with sinker at Base 18 Inverness, fitted with D-4 float for planting at lower levels.

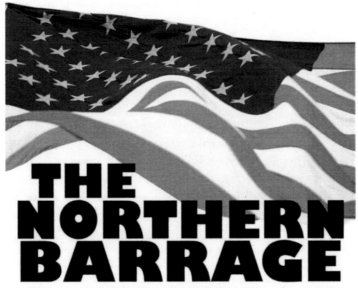

THE NORTHERN BARRAGE

The Fence Across the North Sea in WWI

Editors:
Adrian Harvey
Susan Kruse

INVERNESS LOCAL HISTORY FORUM

Scottish Charity No: SC025287

The Northern Barrage
The Fence Across the North Sea in WWI

Publication © 2020 Inverness Local History Forum

Inverness Local History Forum, Room 2, Spectrum Centre,
1 Margaret Street, Inverness IV1 1SL

Designed and produced by Hargus Ltd, Inverness

Printed by For The Right Reasons, 34-40 Grant Street, Inverness IV3 8BN

Contributing Writers
Inverness Local History Forum:
*Dave Conner, Maureen T Kenyon, Allan Cameron,
Anne C MacKintosh, Adrian Harvey*
Archaeology for Communities in the Highlands (ARCH): *Susan Kruse*
Invergordon Museum & Alness Heritage Centre Dalmore Group:
*Bob Baxter, Alasdair Cameron, Stewart Campbell,
Valerie Campbell-Smith, Catherine Gaston, Alan Kinghorn, Susan Kruse,
Duncan MacLeod, Una McIntosh, Jacky Roberts, Carolyn Samsin,
Malcolm Standring, Ron Stewart*
Groam House Museum: *Ivan Brazier, Barbara Cohen,
Don Holding, Richard Jenner, Janet Witheridge, Robin Witheridge*

ISBN 978-0-9548206-4-0

Front cover
US Mine Squadron One at sea (www.history.navy.mil)
Assembled mines and anchors in Base 18 storage shed (www.history.navy.mil)

Back cover
The U-boat SM U-139 *of the German Kaiserliche Marine* (www.uboat.net)
Map of the Northern Barrage (ILHF based on Admiralty map)
The USS Housatonic *of Mine Squadron One* (Anon.1919)
Unidentified US Navy rating (Andrew Paterson © SHPA)
The American flag raised at Dalmore Distillery (Wayne Abbott © Invergordon Museum)

*The Forum Committee would like to thank Heritage
Lottery Fund (now National Lottery Heritage Fund)
and Inverness Common Good Fund for their support.*

Contents

Andrew Paterson © SHPA

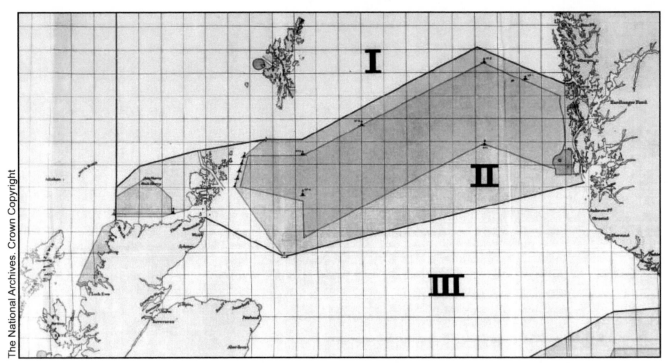

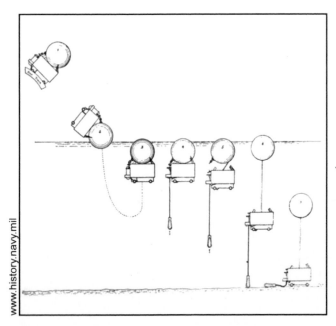

Admiralty Chart from February 1919 showing the minefield in the dark area.

*The reason for the North Sea mine barrage. **SM U-139** shows how advanced the German ocean-going submarines were. She was 2,000 tons displacement, 301 feet long, had a range of 17,700nm at eight knots surfaced and could manage up to 15 knots surfaced and eight submerged. She had four bow tubes, two stern tubes, two 15cm guns (5.9 inch), two 8.8cm guns (3.5 inch) and carried 24 x 21-inch torpedoes, 980 rounds of 15cm shells and 200 rounds of 8.8cm. Her crew of six officers and 56 men allowed enough to form a prize crew if a vessel was captured.*[1]

To combat the U-boat menace the US Navy devised a new style of sea mine; necessary because of the considerable depth (and variation of depths) involved in the North Sea. The Mark VI mine was a 34 inch diameter steel sphere which contained a buoyancy chamber and 300lb of explosive.

The mine featured a long antenna hanging down from the line. Contact with that wire, at whatever depth, would detonate the mine, and likely set off others around. It was not totally foolproof and with care a U-boat might manage to avoid one but the idea was to deter them from trying, or at least damage and bring them to the surface.

The drawing shows the sequence of operations after a mine is launched.[2]

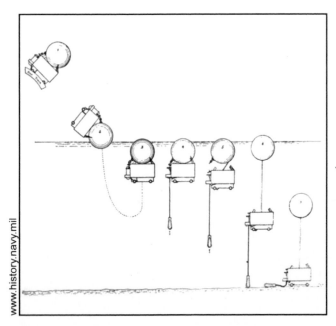

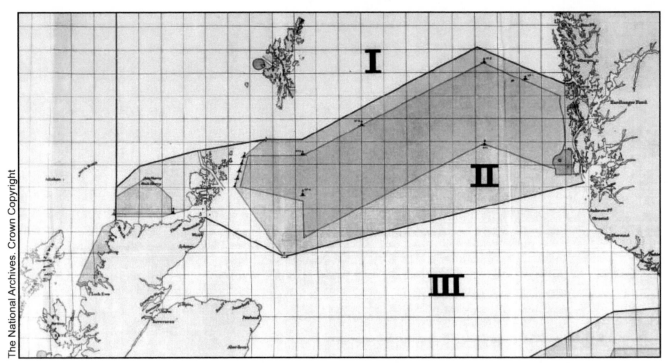

6

1. Introduction

The minefield across the North Sea laid between Orkney and Norway in 1918 was by far the largest undertaking of its kind and became known as the Northern Barrage. It was a joint undertaking by the Royal Navy (RN) and the United States Navy (USN) with 70,117 mines laid by the time the Armistice stopped operations; 56,571 were laid by the USN against 13,546 by the RN.[3]

A minefield to close off the Atlantic exit from the North Sea was formally raised by the USN on 9 May 1917.[4] This became the main USN proposal to the British Admiralty in 1917.[5] It was a proposal which involved massive US expenditure and industrial output.

To make the plan work, the USN would convert eight ships[6] into fast mine layers and develop a cargo fleet of 24[7] ships to transport mine components across the Atlantic. They would also build a factory to produce the explosive and charge the mine casings in the USA. Two large assembly plants would be built in Scotland and they would develop a totally new type of mine (so advanced it was still in the US military inventory during the Vietnam War), and then ordered 100,000 mines before the first one had even been tested.

The Boston-New York passenger liner Massachusetts *which became the* USS Shawmut, *an example of one of the eight liners converted in Boston shipyards into navy minelayers.*

What drove the US Navy to propose this radical plan?

The USS Shawmut *(left) with* HMS Vampire *making a smoke screen.*

The Battle of Jutland in 1916 had been indecisive but it caused the High Seas Fleet of the Imperial German Navy (Kaiserliche Marine - KM) to remain in their North Sea bases for the rest of the war.[8]

It was the KM's submarine arm that would have to fight the war in the Atlantic and try to starve Britain into surrender. During the First World War, the KM had 375 U-boats which sank around 7,663 merchant ships totalling over 15 million tons.[9]

On 1 February 1917 the German government took a large gamble and began unrestricted submarine warfare, sinking ships of belligerent and neutral nations. The gamble was that they would starve Britain before the US could enter the war. By 21 March 1917, seven US merchant ships had been sunk and the USA declared war on Germany on 6 April — the month when 545, 282 gross tons of British shipping was sunk from a total of 881,207 gross tons.[10]

One ship in every four leaving British ports was sunk, and at one time, despite rationing, there was less than one month's wheat supply left in the country.[11]

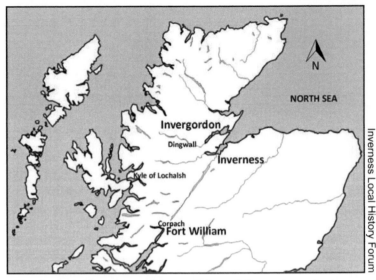

Equipment for Base 18 was shipped from America to Corpach at the head of Loch Linnhe and equipment for Base 17 was landed at Kyle of Lochalsh.

Effective convoy systems, better allied equipment and tactics started to reduce losses and the Dover Barrage was improved in late 1917 to restrict access to the Atlantic via the Straits of Dover. The North Sea access remained largely open, but keen to have a major role and to help protect troop ships as well as commerce, the USN proposed the Northern Barrage. By late 1917, the scheme had been given the green light and the first signs in the Highlands occurred in October when the Captain Lockhart Leith Committee surveyed and reported on the 'Northern Bases'.[12]

The report was very detailed and proposed that mine components shipped from the USA would be received at Corpach and the Kyle of Lochalsh.

The Corpach components would be taken by barge along the Caledonian Canal to an assembly plant based around the Glen Albyn distillery at Muirtown. Once assembled, the mines would be loaded onto barges and transferred to the mine laying ships in the Kessock Roads and Inverness Firth.

Captain Reginald Rowan Belknap USN
Commander of US Mine Squadron One

Captain Reginald Belknap (1871-1959) received numerous commendations for his successful leadership of the US Mine Squadron. Following the First World War, CNO Benson reported that "Captain Belknap deserves, in the opinion of the Chief of Naval Operations, more credit for the success of this undertaking than any other man."

He had served in the Spanish-American War, Boxer Rebellion, and Philippine-American War. He gained distinction in 1909 for his relief work in Italy after the 1908 Messina earthquake and tsunami. He was also a published author, an inventor, a member of many professional and social organisations, and of the Episcopal Church. Belknap was transferred to the retired list in June 1926, but remained on active duty, and in May 1927 was promoted to rear admiral by an act of the US Congress for his Great War service.

The components landed at Kyle would be taken by rail to an assembly plant at the Dalmore distillery and once assembled the mines would be taken by rail to Invergordon to be transferred to barges and then to mine laying ships moored in the Cromarty Firth.

Four days after the Lockhart Leith Committee submitted its report a conference was convened at the Admiralty to decide the way ahead.

The report was agreed and swift action taken. Commanders OG Murfin[13] and TL Johnson USN were dispatched from the USA with authority to speak for the Bureau of Ordnance arriving in London on 23 November 1917.[14]

The Navy Department designated Inverness as Base 18 (see Chapter 2) and Invergordon as Base 17 (see Chapter 3).[15] The bases were prepared by contact through the Admiralty although much material was supplied by the USA.[16] The first draft of men arrived on 27 November 1917. The US national ensign was officially hoisted at Base 18 on 9 February 1918 and at Base 17 on 12 February.

Commander Murfin would be promoted to captain and would command the entire shore establishment consisting of 20 officers and 1,000 enlisted men each at Bases 17 and 18 plus three officers and 60 enlisted men each at Kyle and Corpach.[17]

In addition, there was a USN Base Hospital with 1,000 beds located at Strathpeffer (see Chapter 5).[18]

Rear Admiral Joseph Strauss USN

Rear Admiral Joseph Strauss (1861-1948) was awarded the Distinguished Service Medal for both the laying of the Northern Barrage and its subsequent sweeping.

He went on to become a four-star admiral and Commander-in-Chief of the Asiatic Fleet.

Captain Howard Fiennes Julius Rowley RN

Local support was provided by Captain HFJ Rowley (1868-1948) who was the Senior Naval Officer, Inverness and who took charge of the operations to prepare and defend the firth.

Captain, actually acting-captain, Rowley was a busy man. He was the Senior Naval Officer and Divisional Naval Transport Officer, Inverness from 16 December 1914 to 31 December 1918 having been recalled for war duty. What kept him busy were the three 'm's – men, mail and munitions.

Captain Rowley was awarded the CBE on 1 April 1919 and the US Distinguished Service Medal on 16 December 1919.

He went on to become the RNLI Chief Inspector of Lifeboats from 1919 to 1930 and played a large part in the mechanisation of lifeboat launching. Usefully for us, Captain Rowley was also a keen photographer and his collection is in the Imperial War Museum.

www.history.navy.mil

Unloading unassembled mine case spheres, known as 'eggs'.

The Mine Squadron (the fleet of 10 mine layers and four sea-going tugs) came under the command of Captain RR Belknap USN with a total of 208 officers and 3,839 men.[19]

Captain Belknap arrived in the Inverness Firth with the leading group of mine layers ('planters') on 26 May 1918. The Mine Squadron made 13 excursions, the first on 7 June[20] and the last mines were laid on 26 October.[21] The squadron was loaded and ready to go again on 30 October but operations were suspended in anticipation of the end of hostilities.[22]

Following the Armistice came the massive operation to sweep the area and clear the minefields, where only 42.7 per cent of those that had been laid successfully were recovered.[23]

www.history.navy.mil

The US Mine Squadron One on a minelaying expedition in the North Sea. Steaming in two parallel columns of four are, on the left, USS Saranac, USS Roanoke, USS Housatonic *and* USS Shawmut. *Right column,* USS Canandaigua, USS Canonicus, USS Quinnebaug *and* USS Baltimore.

Assembly Bay for testing and adjusting mines, US Navy Base 18, Inverness.

Dumb (towed) lighter loaded with assembled mines, US Navy Base 18.

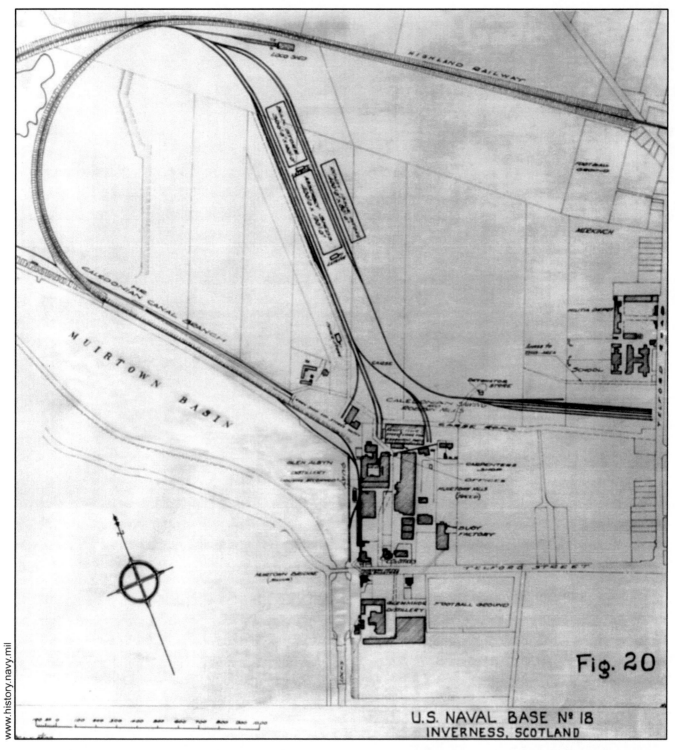

Contemporary plan of US Navy Base 18, Inverness, covering what is now the Carse Industrial Estate. Base 18 was established in, and on land adjoining, the Glen Albyn Distillery premises at Muirtown Bridge near the eastern terminal of the Caledonian Canal, one mile from Inverness.

2. US Navy Base 18 Inverness

Carse Road in Inverness is today a quiet street, running from Telford Road between the terraced Council houses on one side and the Merkinch School on the other, down to the Industrial Estate and Telford Retail Park.

In June 1917 it would have been even quieter, just a narrow thoroughfare between the school garden and fields leading to the sawing and bobbin mills to the rear of the Glen Albyn Distillery and thence to Carse Farm, whose fields occupied all of what is now the Carse Industrial Estate.

A mid-1950s aerial view of the Glen Mhor Distillery (foreground) and the Glen Albyn Distillery beyond on the Muirtown Basin and Caledonian Canal. The building to the left of the large building on Telford Street was the initial headquarters of Base 18.

However, six months on from that, you simply would not have been able to access what is now Carse Road, as a massive security fence topped with barbed wire would have barred your way. Not only that but your very presence in the area would have alerted a man in naval uniform armed with a bayonet-tipped rifle, and in an unmistakable American accent would have asked in no uncertain terms as to your purpose. Because by November 1917, US Navy Base 18 had been established there.

The buildings were requisitioned by the Admiralty and 3,000 barrels of bonded whisky were transferred to the neighbouring Glen Mhor Distillery for safe keeping, and the Navy occupied the buildings as dormitories and for other purposes necessary for the running of a military base. Conversion of the three-storey granaries and other quayside buildings was begun, with the upper floors converted into dormitories and the ground floor turned into a mess-room.[1]
The ground floor of one of the quayside buildings, 70 feet long by 50 feet wide, was adapted for use as a motor garage, general stores and canteen. The bonded store, measuring 190 feet by 94 feet and containing two floors, was converted into a store for sinkers, component parts, clothing and general stores. The sinkers were stored on the lower floor where 3,300 feet of narrow gauge railway track was laid down, providing accommodation for 1,000 units.[2]

The first American staff and equipment arrived at Inverness on 8 January 1918. The Base HQ was initially the Distillery Managing Director's house on Telford Street, where the Stars and Stripes was ceremonially raised in February 1918.

The staff eventually formed a US Mine Force of over 1,000 officers and men. The Glen Albyn Distillery housed accommodation and the requisitioned Muirtown Hotel, alongside Muirtown Bridge, became the sick bay for the base.

Anon 1919 p86

The Stars and Stripes flies over the Base 18 headquarters in the Distillery Managing Director's house on Telford Street.

The Carse area had been rapidly set up as a construction base complete with its own railway system, based upon the single line branch from the North Line to Muirtown Basin. The amount of railway tracks installed was phenomenal, especially given the short time-scale involved. They covered the whole of what is now the Industrial Estate with a string of holding sidings stretching along what is now Carse Road and taking up all of what later became the Merkinch School playing fields.

On 25 January 1918 the Headmaster of the Merkinch School had been interviewed by the British Naval Authorities enquiring as to what accommodation could be made available for the billeting of men of the American Navy, in connection with work which would be going ahead in the fields adjoining the school.

It was agreed to make the Infant Department available as a temporary billet and the pupils were transferred to the main school on Monday 4 February.[3]

www.history.navy.mil

Adrian Harvey

The Sick Bay at 90 Telford Street, the former Muirtown Hotel. It is one of the few buildings used by the US Navy in Inverness which still survives, seen here in April 2020.

Following the Easter holidays on 9 April, by which time huts had been erected to accommodate the US Naval servicemen, the infants returned to their school.

(Before they left Inverness in 1919, the Americans gave a great big party and concert in the Rose Street Drill Hall, Inverness. Pupils aged over eight from various town schools were entertained and a huge Christmas tree laden with gifts was erected. The US Navy also presented the Merkinch Primary School with money to purchase playground equipment.)[4]

By 26 April 1918 the vast preparations were almost complete. What had been the school garden had been turned into a large railway siding with the whole area between the school and the canal enclosed with a barbed wire fence manned by armed sentries. Here the assembled mines were stored, before being taken by rail to the Muirtown Quay and transferred to lighters.

The Merkinch School billet on Telford Road (from a 1906 postcard).

A brass plaque commemorating the stay of the men of Base 18 is mounted within the school.

Assembled mines stored on the fields next to Merkinch School.

The Base 18 barracks in the grounds of Glen Albyn Distillery.

The Base 18 mine assembly sheds from the perimeter. The whole area, including the distillery property, was enclosed by a seven foot high, 3,200 yard long fence.[5]

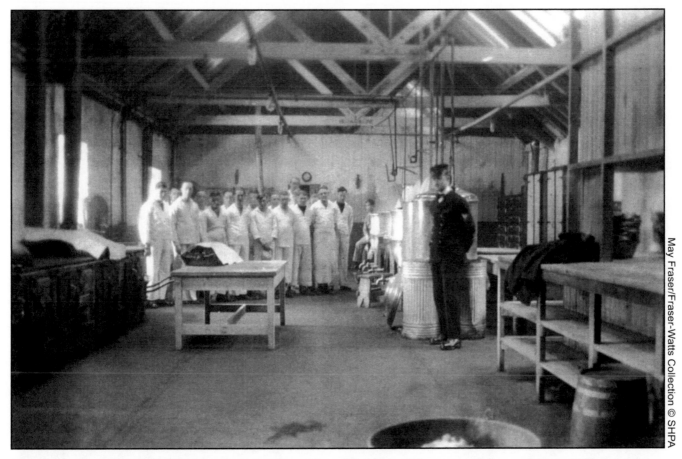

This is the interior of the kitchen area in Glen Albyn Distillery. The ground floor of the buildings were below sewer level, so all kitchen and sanitary accommodation was placed on the first floor. The United States supplied a battleship cooking outfit.[6]

Base 18 opens for business...the first flag being hoisted at the former residence of the Glen Albyn Distillery Managing Director in Inverness on 9 February 1918.

The Mine Force commander Rear Admiral Joseph Strauss and his staff.

Squadron Captains standing from left; BL Canaga, TL Johnson, JH Tomb, JW Greenslade, S Gannon, WH Reynolds and DP Mannix. Seated; WT Cluverius, CD Stearns, RR Belknap, HF Butler and AW Marshall.

A US Navy band marching across the swing bridge over the Caledonian Canal, with Glen Mhor Distillery in the background. The sign reads 'Dead Slow. Barrier.'

Commander, Mine Force and Staff at Inverness in 1918. Captain Orin G Murfin, Rear Admiral Joseph Strauss, Lieutenant JG Robert N. Smither, Lieutenant Thomas Newhall, unidentified, Commander Eugene J Grow MC.

Admiral Henry Thomas Mayo USN
Commander in Chief Atlantic Fleet

Admiral Henry Thomas Mayo (1856-1937), Commander in Chief, Atlantic Fleet, shown here with Mine Force Commander Rear Admiral Joseph Strauss. In the early 1900s Mayo was an aide to Secretary of the Navy Daniels.

Appointed Vice Admiral in June 1915, and as the new Commander in Chief, Atlantic Fleet, Mayo received the rank of Admiral in June 1916. For his organisation and support of First World War US Naval Forces both in American and European waters, he was awarded the Navy Distinguished Service Medal and various foreign decorations. He later evidenced foresight in urging the postwar development of fleet aviation.

Prior to the establishment of Base 18 the Caledonian Canal had been used for day traffic only; consequently, in order that traffic through the canal might be continued day and night, the provision of navigation lights was undertaken — 32-piled erections were constructed and the Northern Lights Commissioners provided 32 lights of the compressed oil gas type.

Four illuminated signal boards and two railway signals were also supplied. To accommodate the increased personnel required to work the lock gates and canal bridges, various sheds and buildings on the route of the canal and at Banavie railway station were requisitioned and fitted up as quarters. In all, accommodation was provided for about 250 men.[7]

Mine barges in Clachnaharry locks of the Caledonian Canal.

On arrival at Muirtown Quay, the mines were offloaded from the lighters into railway trucks and conveyed into the depot. The mines were delivered on the west side of the assembly shed and after passing through the shed from west to east, during which they were examined and tested, they were stored in the ready issue shed.[8]

To the north of the distillery premises an area of about 45 acres was taken over by the Admiralty for the erection of an assembly shed (above), a ready issue shed, a bulk store, and other buildings (see map on page 12).

The assembly shed, 400 feet by 100 feet, and the ready issue shed, 400 feet by 80 feet and each 11 feet in height, were constructed of steel framing covered with corrugated steel sheets. They were constructed in bays of 25 feet. The assembly shed was steam heated, the boilers being placed in a steel framed building adjoining. The ready issue shed had accommodation for about 2,700 mines.[9]

Unloading mine sinkers at the assembly sheds.

Mine sinkers stored two deep, and to the rear, mine spheres stored three deep, awaiting assembly, or 'marrying'.

Mine sinkers move along the assembly bay anchor track.

23

Unassembled mine case spheres in the bulk storeroom. Measuring 300 feet by 100 feet and 11 feet in height, it was constructed of home-grown timber framing and covered with corrugated steel sheets with a concrete floor.[10]

Handling the mine cases by wheeling the spheres from the bulk store to the assembly shed.

One of the bays in the assembly sheds at Base 18 where the component parts were brought in at the far end of the bay. By the time they traversed the shed they were completed units.

Testing and adjusting the firing mechanism of the Mark VI Mine. The success of the Northern Barrage was largely dependent on preserving the secrecy of this mechanism. The virtue of the copper wire or antenna was that it could be deployed by its own float (submerged) so that the ship or submarine would not have to hit the mine — it could merely run into the wire but would still be within lethal range of the explosion. The electrolytic firing influence was called the K-device, and when the steel hull of a ship made contact with the copper antenna wire, the steel became one electrode of an electrolytic cell connected by the wire to the copper plates which became the other electrode. A current then flowed through the antenna wire with the return path being the sea water itself. This small current closed the sensitive relay which connected the firing battery to the electric detonator.[11]

Mark VI mine with sinker.

Mine fitted with balsa floats for planting at shallow depths.

Assembled mines and anchors in the ready issue store, awaiting the return of the Mine Squadron, prior to loading for the succeeding operation.

Loading the assembled mines into the wagons.

Trainload of mines ready for transportation to the quay and the waiting mine lighters. The locomotive shed was 85 feet long by 25 feet wide, steel framed and covered with steel sheets. It was capable of housing four locomotives.[12]

Mines loaded on wagons for transportation to the quay. Three and one quarter miles of standard railway track were laid, connecting with the Caledonian Canal branch of the Highland Railway Company's system at Muirtown Basin. In addition, two and one half miles of narrow gauge railway and half a mile of new roadway were constructed.[13]

After the mines were assembled on the production lines in the Base 18 sheds, they were placed in trainloads in the holding sidings until needed and then returned by rail to the Muirtown Basin. They were then loaded back on to lighters/barges and taken via the Clachnaharry sea lock into the Beauly Firth where the Minelaying Squadron awaited. To ensure that these big ships could safely navigate as far as possible up the Firth and enable transshipment off Clachnaharry, the Firth had been dredged. The work followed the natural channel that runs from Chanonry Point to close to Kilmuir through the two sandbanks known as Middle Bank and Meikle Mee; hence the term still referred to locally as 'The Yankee Channel' (see page 54).

Loading mines for transportation in the Muirtown Basin alongside Glen Albyn Distillery.

The loading basin for Base 18 on the Caledonian Canal, showing how the lighters were loaded to transfer the mines to the mine layers. Two oil tanks for the supply of fuel oil to the motor lighters were erected on the quay at the south end of the distillery.[14]

US Navy officers.

On the following pages are some of the faces of the men who worked on the Northern Barrage, taken by the Andrew Paterson Photographic Studio in Academy Street, Inverness.

Andrew Paterson (1877-1948) was a local but internationally acclaimed portrait photographer who entertained officers and men from the US Navy, the British armed forces and the Australian army at his home in Culduthel Road.[15]

The unidentified naval officer at right is part of the group in the below photograph taken at the Inverness home of Andrew Paterson.

Four US Navy officers with Andrew Paterson and his family at Tigh-an-Uillt, *in Culduthel Road. Mrs Jean Paterson and daughter Constance flank the group with twin sons Hamish and Hector in the centre. Hector, holding the family Scottish terrier, Loos, would take over the operation of the studio upon his father's death in 1948 until his own retirement in 1980.*

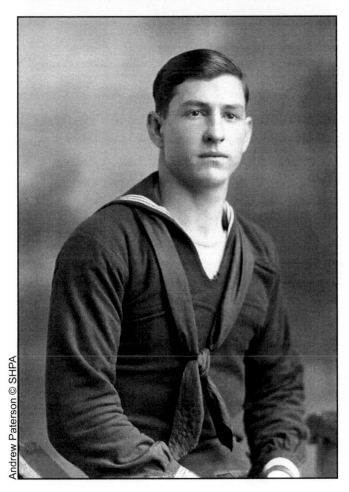

So what effect did the American Navy have on Inverness? Well, most young Inverness men were away fighting and it was a fertile location for the young American matelots, both those working in Base 18 and those serving on the Minelayer Squadron which was based in the Beauly Firth. Their presence attracted many local ladies, and many a romance began — some of which culminated in the ladies becoming US Navy Brides and subsequently moving to the USA (see Chapter 6).

There was a considerable amount of getting together between the local military bosses, the public and the Americans. Locals were frequently entertained by various bands raised from the US Navy personnel and as Base 18 was located on Telford Street across from the Caley Park, the naval hierarchy encouraged their men to let off steam on the sports field rather than in the local pubs. Some previously unknown (to Invernessians anyway) sports were played there, doubtless to the amazement of the locals.

www.history.navy.mil

Men marching to noon mess after a hard morning's work, September 1918.

At the war's end many Americans left Inverness for demobilisation, but following the Armistice came the clean-up operation to deal with the minefield which in peacetime was now a considerable hazard to shipping. Mine Squadron One transferred over 400 men to the bases prior to sailing for home on 30 November 1918 and the *Black Hawk* moved to Kirkwall on 4 January 1919 until 25 November 1919. Twelve new mine sweepers and six sub-chasers were sent over from the US to perform the joint sweeping operations between 29 April and 30 September 1919 (see Chapter 9).

Although much more dangerous than mine laying, the removal and destruction of the mines proved a faster exercise and the base itself was dismantled and much of it taken back to the United States (albeit there are possibly still souvenirs around the town).

The Carse returned to its previous tranquil existence, once the fences and barbed wire came down. The area which had been a hive of industry for a year or so was now quiet again and most of the signs of the base's existence are long gone. Even the Canal Branch railway line has gone although it did continue to be occasionally used up until the 1960s. Its memory lives on however, as the line of the former track-bed forms the curve which marks the western extremity of the land on the Carse.

The distilleries are also now only memories, as is the Caley Park — in fact the only buildings still standing in the area which were there in 1918 are 90 Telford Street (the former Muirtown Hotel, the two distillery cottages on Carse Road (next to the rear of the Co-op Supermarket) and the Merkinch School, although there is now (2020) a brand new school building occupying part of the former 'sidings' area of the school garden/playing field.

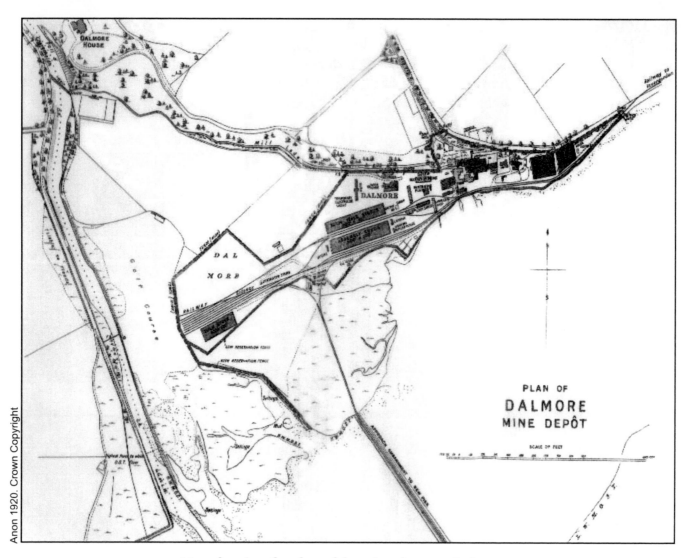

Map showing the plan of the mine depot at Dalmore.

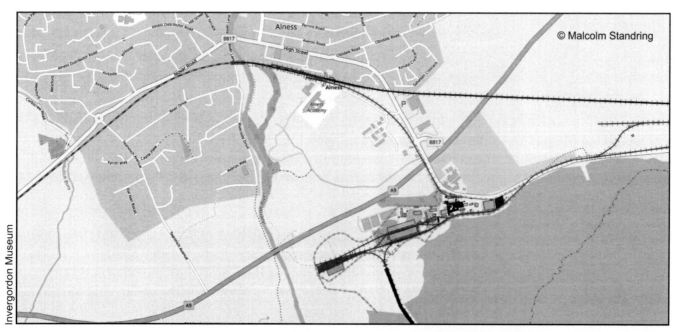

Modern map showing US Base 17 layout in relation to present day.
Contains OS data © Crown Copyright and database right (2019)

3. US Navy Base 17 Dalmore

The Royal Navy moved into Dalmore Distillery on the northern shore of the Cromarty Firth approximately two and one half miles from Invergordon in preparation for the American arrival of minelaying staff. The first stores arrived for Overseas Mine Bases 17 and 18 on 20 January 1918.[1] On 25-26 May, Mine Squadron One arrived in Scotland. Three mine laying ships and a collier were deployed to the Cromarty Firth.[2]

The northern of the two minelaying bases, Dalmore was situated on the east coast, with the Cromarty Firth providing deep water access and ease of movement under the protective services of the Royal Navy fleet situated at Invergordon. The base was also sometimes referred to as Base 17 Invergordon.

The problem of shipping components and supplies from the States was solved by landing the essentials on the west coast as this was safer that sailing around the northern most point of Scotland avoiding U-boat activity.

The US flag at Dalmore was raised on 12 February 1918, three days after Inverness.[3]

Group photo at Dunrobin Castle of the Yankee Mining Squadron US Base 17 when they first arrived.

Base 17 officers and staff. From left; WJ Thomas, Lieutenant CL Austin, LM Stewart, AA Booth, Lieutenant JGMM Scaley, T Saul, EA Walleson, P Ferguson, Lieutenant HH Foy and Lieutenant WA Preslin.

Officers were billeted at Dalmore House which offered tennis courts and a golf course nearby and was within walking distance of the site.

Wayne O Abbott USN

Most of the photographs used in this chapter are from the Wayne Abbott Collection (© Invergordon Museum). Some of his photographs have notations on the reverse side, and are quoted in some instances below. Some of the photos were posted home to his grandmother whom he lived with. Copies of the family photos were given to the museum by his grandson, John Bowen in 2018. John and his wife visited from the United States to trace his grandfather's journey.

Wayne Abbot aged 20. The caption on the reverse reads: "Nov 17, 1918. To Grandmother from Wayne, Base Seventeen, U.S. Naval Forces, European waters, c/o Postmaster N.Y."

Once components reached Dalmore, the process of unloading, storing, assembling and then placing completed mines onto railway wagons for loading onto lighters was similar as at Base 18, discussed above pp 22-28.

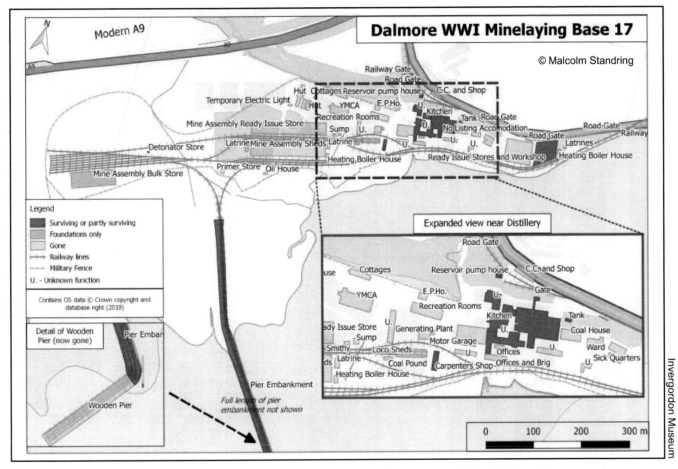

Dalmore WWI Minelaying Base 17

Dalmore, with its large warehouses was an ideal location, and the field to the west of the distillery had three large warehouses erected for assembling and storing parts.

The freight yard had a number of sidings. The large bulk store warehouse can be seen at the rear on the left. Its foundations can still be traced in places. The small arrowed building to the rear is the detonator store.

The detonator store is the only surviving First World War building on this site, shown here in January 2020. All other structures in this field date from the Second World War.

Aerial photograph of Base 17, taken from a British airship. Note the camouflage roofs.

Dalmore

Modern aerial photograph January 2020.

Components destined for Base 17 in Dalmore arrived at Kyle of Lochalsh and were then transported east by the Highland Railway Company.

Extensive alterations and extensions were needed to the pier at Kyle, as well as extra gun emplacements at Kyleakin on Skye, with searchlights to protect the station across the Minch. Rail traffic on the Kyle railway line was reduced to one train a day, and a new passing place was constructed.[4] Engines and coal wagons were borrowed from the London & South Western Railway and the South Eastern & Chatham railway, and brake vans from others.[5]

The transportation of goods to Dalmore required a new branch line to go direct into the distillery, as well as numerous sidings. In total 7.5 miles of standard gauge railway was constructed as well as 3.75 miles of narrow gauge railway around the sheds.[6]

In addition, a new line was built from the distillery along the shore to Invergordon for completed mines to be transported to vessels.[7] The mainline was heavily used, so did not have capacity for extra traffic.[8]

Railway crane at Dalmore.

Wayne Abbott Collection © Invergordon Museum

Trains ran on this shore line three or four times daily carrying the mines to the Admiralty pier in Invergordon, where they were then loaded onto lighters to take out to the mine laying vessels moored in the Cromarty Firth.[9]

The Buckie & Keith branch line rails were lifted to provide the extra track needed for all this activity. Engines and wagons were borrowed from various companies.[10]

The connection from the mainline to the new railway at Belleport Junction was dismantled probably shortly after the war ended. However, hints of its route could be traced on aerial photographs from the 1950s. There was a spur on this new branch, which may have served for marshalling or as an 'escape' to protect the Dalmore site in case of a runaway. The route of the branch passed through the present-day copse, east of the water treatment plant, then very close to Belleport House, crossed the former A9 (now the B817), and entered the Dalmore Distillery site at the east gate. A 2019 walkover survey found a seven metre length of the track still in situ (see maps on pages 36 and 50).[11]

Researchers Stewart Campbell and Bob Baxter uncovered a portion of rail track from the connection to the main line in 2019.

Bob Baxter

Before the Americans arrived a British naval detail was sent to move some 300,000 gallons of whisky to other distilleries. Some of the barrels were transported on the newly laid railway line to Invergordon harbour while other consignments went by lorry. All were accompanied by an excise officer, but even so some ratings found that by pressing the barrels the staves would open and whisky could be leaked from the casks into buckets.[12]

The front row of the assembly sheds in December 1918. To the left (west) of these sheds was the bulk store where mine components were stored. After assembly, the mines were transported on open railway wagons and taken to Invergordon Pier to be loaded onto lighters and transferred to planters ready for the convoy to mine laying areas. Note the brussels sprouts growing in the foreground.

Stone distillery buildings were taken over as accommodation blocks. Wayne Abbott marked his block with a tick. Note the camouflage paint on the left added to one of the distillery buildings.

The building on the left is the carpenters' shop which was part of the distillery. Behind is a railway carriage on one of the spur lines similar to the lines at the front of the photograph which lead to the main line. To the right is an old distillery shed, function unknown. The larger building at the rear is recorded as being the recreation rooms. There is a raised pipeline running between this building and the main distillery building. The small shed is part of the water feeding system for the distillery. The low boundary fence can also be seen at the back.

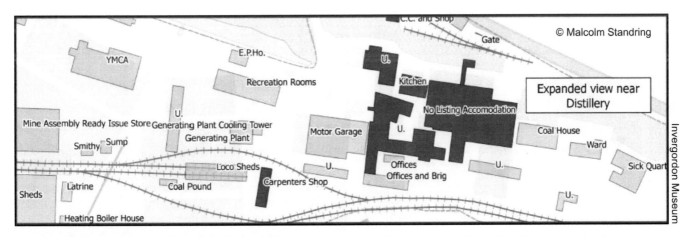

An enlargement of the map featured on page 39 to reference it against the photograph above. The darker shade buildings still survive.
Contains OS data © Crown Copyright and database right (2019)

The YMCA building at Dalmore Distillery in September 1918. It was used extensively for recreation purposes including sports games, dances and other events.

"The rear of our YMCA hut. The fellows who first came to the base built the hut." Wayne Abbott's caption to the above photograph, which shows the distillery cottages on the left. The recreation huts are behind the YMCA and the camouflaged building is the generator building. The chimneys of the distillery still exist.

Interaction and acceptance by the local population was crucial to a harmonious life as shown by this snowball fight with local children. Wayne Abbott is the sailor on the left holding the snowball.

Safety was an important factor at such a volatile site so a fire engine was a priority along with a staffed emergency sick bay. The fire engine was a Merryweather Astor which was used at Dalmore until 1923 when it was sold for £60.[13]

The new galley kitchen in the foreground which caught fire in 1919.

"This is the brig, in other words where the prisoners are kept."
Caption by Wayne Abbott; the garage and truck pool is on the left.

A large number of sidings were needed to move components and finished mines, with mobile cranes to lift them.

47

"One of our Chief Petty Officers sitting on a mine egg and beside two mine egg anchors. This is in front of one of the shops where we assemble mines." Caption by Wayne Abbott.

Wayne Abbot was amazed at how small the railway bogies were in Scotland. "One of Great Britain's largest box cars" he wrote on the back of this photograph.

"A couple of eggs at Base 17." Caption by Wayne Abbott.

Discharging mines to the base.

Mine Storage Sheds.

In transit to the lighters.

The loading pier at Invergordon.

Lighters at Invergordon.

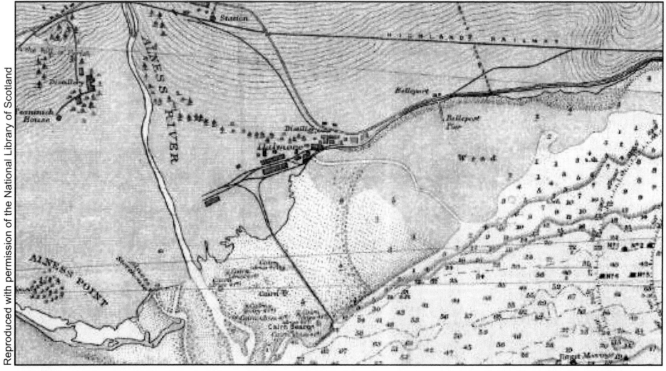

Admiralty chart from 1921 showing the pier. It also shows the railway links from the mainline.

At first all completed mines were transported by rail to Invergordon for launching from the Admiralty Pier. This was seen as a temporary measure, until a pier could be constructed at Dalmore. The long embankment required tons of fill, on which two railway lines were laid, and the pier at the end was constructed of timber; the total cost being £114,000.[14] It was not complete by the end of the war, but when later finished it became known as the Yankee Pier. The wooden pier was demolished in 1924[15], but the rest was in use again during the Second World War. Much of it still survives today.

All that remains of the Yankee Pier in January 2020. The structure at the end dates from the Second World War.

US personnel attended churches in the community, but there was no Roman Catholic church in the area. They constructed a Roman Catholic chapel in Invergordon on waste ground at the top of Invergordon High Street, opposite Invergordon Museum. The church was used until the late 1950s when it was replaced by a Nissen hut near the Invergordon railway station.

A similar organ to the one pictured above was donated by the Americans to the Alness United Free Church, now the derelict old Church of Scotland building. It can be seen at Alness Heritage Centre.

*The Beauly basin from the hills above North Kessock, showing the
Inverness harbour entrance and the ferry slipway at South Kessock.*

Ships at anchor in the Beauly Firth opposite North Kessock.

4. Defending Base 18

The Inverness Firth is relatively shallow and there were neither prepared anchorages nor military defences for the approaches to Inverness. This became a major concern after Inverness was selected as a busy anchorage for the US Navy mine-laying fleet, due to arrive in 1918. A major report was prepared by the Lockhart Leith Committee on 26 October 1917.[1]

Regarding anchorage for ships in the Inverness Firth, the report stated:

"32. Anchorage for Ships

(a) Inverness Firth. It should be noted that Inverness Firth is not defended, but attack from Submarine in the Firth itself does not appear likely.

(b) Kessock Road. Eastern end of Beauly Basin. If moorings are laid down there is room in Kessock Road for 4 Light Cruisers or 12 Destroyers (say two at a buoy). This anchorage is strongly recommended as it would save barges and towing.

(c) It is for consideration whether moorings should be laid down as convenient in Inverness Firth between Fortrose and Munlochy Bay. The nearer ships can get to the Assembly Depot the quicker will be the transport.

33. The Channel should be buoyed from Fort George to Kessock Road with light buoys.

34. It will be necessary to dredge the Channel off the Meikle Mee bank to at least a depth of 16 feet to allow ships to reach Kessock Road at all states of the tide.

35. It will be necessary to keep an Oiler in Inverness Firth for the use of HM Ships working from there."[2]

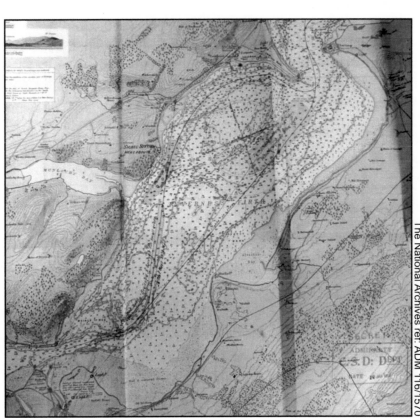

This annotated chart from the National Archives in Kew, shows the planned measures for the anchorages and their defence. It includes the desired position of the Signal Station at Castleton Point in Avoch, buoys for the mine-laying vessels and a dredged approach channel. Leading lights and a battery of guns are shown at Chanonry Ness together with a submarine boom to be installed between Fort George and Rosemarkie. Fort George also has a second Signal Station.

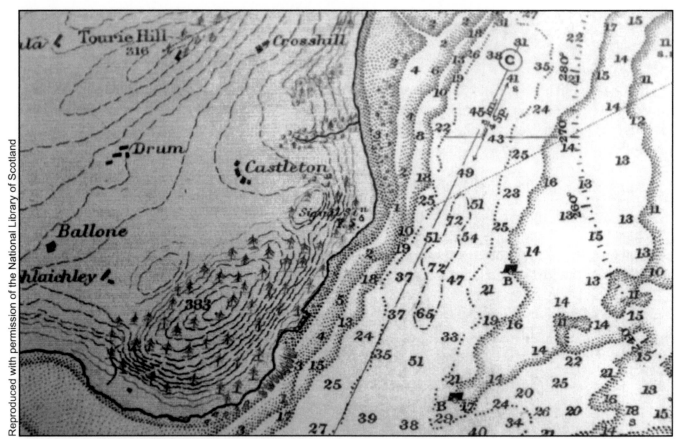

Admiralty Chart 1451 New Edition 5 July 1918. This detail of Castleton Point shows a Signal Station and FS (for Flag Staff) off Castleton. This was built in 1918 to control the movement of shipping and was manned by a Petty Officer from the Coastguard Signal Service and three Signalmen from the RNVR — the Royal Naval Voluntary Reserve. (The names of some of the personnel, Leading Signalmen King, Smith and Knox, are recorded in the local newspaper as hosting a dance in March 1919 in Rosehaugh Hall, Avoch.)

Nothing remains of the Castleton signal station now. The Black Isle District Council minutes relate that Avoch Parish Council wanted first option on the sale of the Signal Station for use as a cottage hospital (or possibly an isolation hospital). However, according to local tradition, after the war the corrugated iron panels from the Signal Station were 'acquired' by two local businessmen and constructed into two sizable sheds on Long Road in Avoch. These have since been dismantled. The chart above shows the position of mooring buoys for use by the US Navy mine-laying fleet.

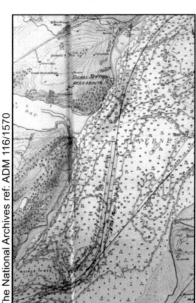

Many fishermen from Avoch knew of a 'Yankee Channel' but its exact location was not known.[3] The map at left shows the planned position of the dredged channel. It reads "Channel being dredged and buoyed for small craft. 18 feet deep at low water."

The 1918 Admiralty Chart 1451 New Edition 5 July 1918 at right shows the actual dredged channel and the lights to mark it.

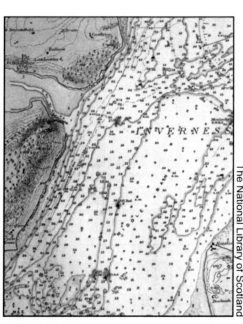

The above photo shows the 15 Pounder Gun Battery on Chanonry Ness. The exact location is unknown. It must have been on the eastern side, somewhere between the golf club house and the lighthouse and with a clear field of fire covering both channels approaching Chanonry Point.

The firth was defended by a new gun emplacement on Chanonry Point. There were two guns in the sandbagged revetments left and right of the fire direction tower which appears to have a speaking tube to each gun position. The guns are BLC 15 pounders, dismounted from their wheels, capable of firing 3-inch shells to about five km. The guns were manned by Royal Marine Artillery ratings who were accommodated, along with a detachment of the Highland Cycle Battalion, in the poorhouse situated on Chanonry Ness. The poorhouse accounts record that the Admiralty paid £105 in 1919/20 for billeting and in 1918 had paid £25 towards improving the drainage having failed to obtain a grant from the council.[4]

The Search Light Battery at Chanonry Point, fitted with 24-inch acetylene search lights and semaphore. Using the background roofs as reference, the location almost certainly lies in the passage through to the dunes between the golf course and the lighthouse boundary wall. It's one of Inverness Senior Naval Officer Captain Rowley's photos and it would be nice to think that he rested his camera on the boundary wall corner to take this shot. There is a lot of detail to examine. For example, the 'sand bagging' seems to be ongoing. The central figure is a bearded man in naval uniform. The six buttons on his jacket indicates he is a senior rating (officers wear eight buttons) and the buttons on the sleeve worn horizontal to the cuff would indicate he is a Chief Petty Officer (three buttons although only two appear to be visible).

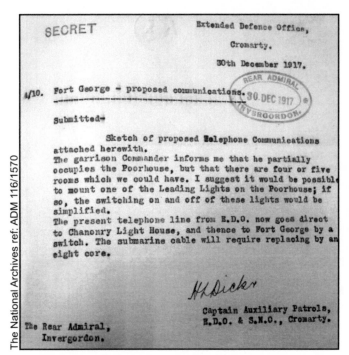

SECRET

Extended Defence Office,
Cromarty.
30th December 1917.

4/10. Fort George - proposed communications.

Submitted-

Sketch of proposed Telephone Communications attached herewith.

The garrison Commander informs me that he partially occupies the Poorhouse, but that there are four or five rooms which we could have. I suggest it would be possible to mount one of the Leading Lights on the Poorhouse; if so, the switching on and off of these lights would be simplified.

The present telephone line from E.D.O. now goes direct to Chanonry Light House, and thence to Fort George by a switch. The submarine cable will require replacing by an eight core.

H.L.Dicks

Captain Auxiliary Patrols,
E.D.O. & S.N.O., Cromarty.

The Rear Admiral,
Invergordon.

The document above from the Extended Defence Office in December 1917 suggested the need to upgrade communications between Chanonry Point and Fort George. Around the same time a submarine boom across the firth was proposed, as indicated in the hand-drawn plan at right.

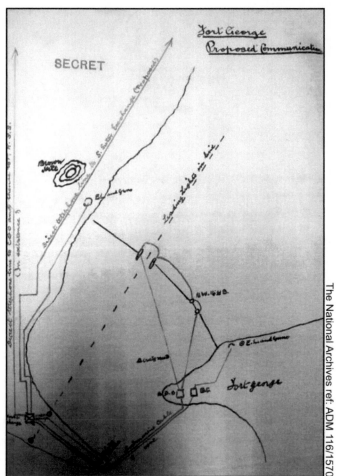

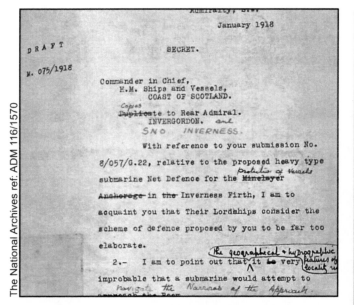

January 1918

DRAFT
M. 075/1918

SECRET.

Commander in Chief,
H.M. Ships and Vessels,
COAST OF SCOTLAND.

Copies
Duplicate to Rear Admiral.
INVERGORDON. and
SNO INVERNESS.

With reference to your submission No. 8/057/G.22, relative to the proposed heavy type submarine Net Defence for the Minelayer Anchorage in the Inverness Firth, I am to acquaint you that Their Lordships consider the scheme of defence proposed by you to be far too elaborate.

2.- I am to point out that it is very improbable that a submarine would attempt to navigate the Narrows of the Approach.

Extract from a letter concerning the plans for the submarine boom. Initial plans were considered too elaborate, but a boom was built with sailing instructions issued on how to pass through it.

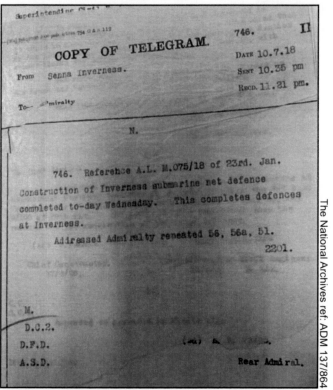

COPY OF TELEGRAM.

746.   II
DATE 10.7.18
SENT 10.35 pm.
RECD. 11.21 pm.

From Senna Inverness.

To   Admiralty

N.

746. Reference A.L. M.075/18 of 23rd. Jan. Construction of Inverness submarine net defence completed to-day Wednesday. This completes defences at Inverness.

Addressed Admiralty repeated 56, 56a, 51.
2201.

M.
D.C.2.
D.F.D.
A.S.D.
                    Rear Admiral.

The completion of the boom was confirmed in this telegram from the Senior Naval Officer Inverness, Captain HFJ Rowley, dated 10 July 1918 — after mine-laying operations had commenced.

There are no pictures of the submarine boom installed between Fort George and Rosemarkie. The above photo was taken from 2,000 feet by CPO A Blackwell RNAS, and shows HMS Penelope entering what must have been a similar arrangement in an unknown location.

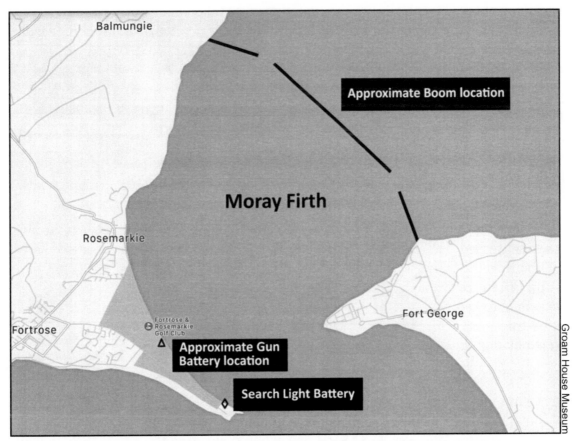

The planned location of the boom. Searches were undertaken in 2018 to try to find the anchor points of the submarine boom. A rock was identified north of Rosemarkie which may have provided anchorage. At Fort George, the Black Scarp rocks could have provided anchorage but concrete from the Second World War period was overlaid on top of any evidence which may have confirmed this. An alternative theory is that the boom was not anchored to the shore but was weighted down and buoyed in shallow water.

No additional protection was needed for Base 17 at Dalmore due to defences of Invergordon in place. Booms were laid between the Sutors to protect the naval port of Invergordon, and gun emplacements on the shores.

All booms constructed for the defence of northern Scotland, including Inverness and Cromarty Firths and Scapa Flow, were manufactured and maintained at the British Boom Defence Net Department in Inverness. These works were located in the disused Thornbush Brewery directly opposite the Thornbush Quay and the Rose Street Foundry shipyard on Kessock Road.[5]

The ground floor of the Thornbush Brewery maltings was taken over by HM Board of Admiralty and it was here that a team of experts under the guidance of Commander Donald J Munro assembled the anti-submarine nets.

These steel nets were suspended below the boom, and were manufactured by the Rose Street Foundry under the direction of Mr Sam Hunter-Gordon.

The rafts which carried them were made in the shipyard and the entire booms were then towed into position by requisitioned fishing vessels.[6]

Admiralty Port Office, Inverness Naval Base. The buildings to the rear form part of the disused Thornbush Brewery.

As the war went on more boom defences were ordered by the Admiralty for various theatres and female labour was called in. After being trained, the women proved just as capable as the men and Admiral Sir Rosslyn Wemyss, First Sea Lord, when inspecting the works in 1916 expressed his wonder at the way they accomplished their tasks.[7]

The manufacture of these defences at the Thornbush lasted right up until the end of the war. The system proved so successful it was used to protect harbours and naval anchorages all over the world.

As part of the defences, the inner firth and Inverness harbour entrance were patrolled by fishing drifters converted into armed naval auxiliaries. The *Lavatera* (above) was built in 1913 by W & G Stephen of Banff for John Wood Snr. With a displacement of 84 GRT, she was requisitioned by the Admiralty for wartime service in the Royal Navy in March 1915, and returned to the owners in 1920. During the Second World War she was again requisitioned in April 1940 until July 1946 and first used as a Barrage Balloon Vessel (BBV) and later as a Harbour Service Vessel. She was scrapped in 1948. In the photograph above the crew are in civilian clothing, and the bow-mounted cannon (a six pounder gun) is clearly visible. She is flying the White Ensign.[8]

The fishing drifter *Clans* (above) was also used as an armed naval auxiliary. She was built in Macduff in 1915 with a displacement of 89 GRT, and requisitioned by the Admiralty for wartime service in June. Returned to the owners in 1919 she was again requisitioned for service in August 1939 until April 1945 as a Harbour Service Vessel. In the photograph above the crew are wearing uniform and she is flying the White Ensign.[9]

An ambulance serving the US Naval Base Hospital in Strathpeffer in 1918.

A hospital case being loaded for the drive to Strathpeffer.

Hospital garages and ambulances in Strathpeffer.

5. US Navy Hospital in Strathpeffer

When the US Navy arrived in the Highlands, there was limited hospital provision, with most military casualties taken by rail to Aberdeen. Although both Base 17 and 18 had sick bays, the US Navy decided that they needed their own hospital facilities. Strathpeffer was the ideal location, situated on the railway roughly halfway between both bases. It had large hotels because of its focus as a spa resort, a good water supply, and was even thought by the Americans to have a "climate...somewhat less severe than that generally prevalent." Strathpeffer became one of four US naval hospitals in Europe, the others being at Leith, Queenstown, Ireland and Brest, in France.[1]

This photo of hospital staff standing at the rear of the Pavilion dates from September 1918. In the background is the Highland Hotel.

Two large hotels, the Highland Hotel owned by the Highland Railway and the large Ben Wyvis Hotel were taken over, and with the Pavilion were able to accommodate between 500 and 1,000 beds and offices.[2]

Raising the flag near the Pavilion.

The ivy-covered Ben Wyvis Hotel which became Hospital Building No.2 in September 1918.

Casualties were taken from trains and transported by ambulance to the hospitals.

British patients were also sent to the hospital here. In 1918 total admissions were 2,182 (777 US Navy, 1,002 Royal Navy, 402 British Army, and one civilian emergency). Of these 1,288 came via British 'ambulance trains'. There were 946 surgical operations performed in Strathpeffer.[3]

The hospital was also used for infectious diseases. Its opening coincided with the outbreak of Spanish Influenza which had a devastating impact on the civilian and military population. In particular, naval ships were vulnerable, and the navy recommended cases to be sent from the ships to Strathpeffer for quarantine.[4]

The Highland Hotel was classified as Hospital Building No.1.

Roseann Christie

Interior scenes within Building No.1, the Highland Hotel.

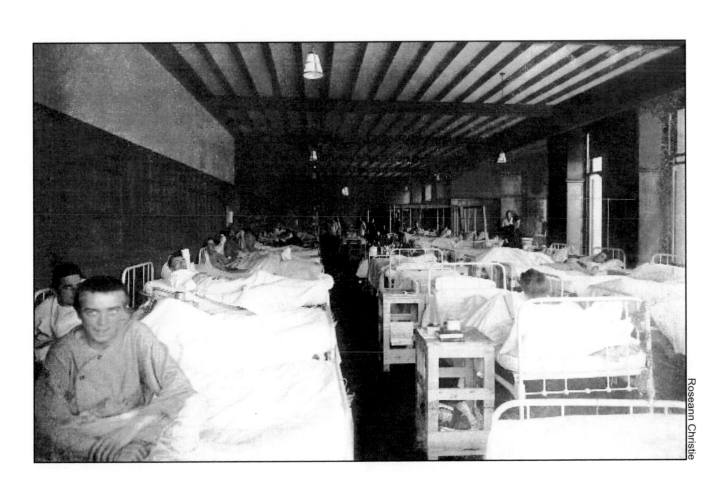

Roseann Christie

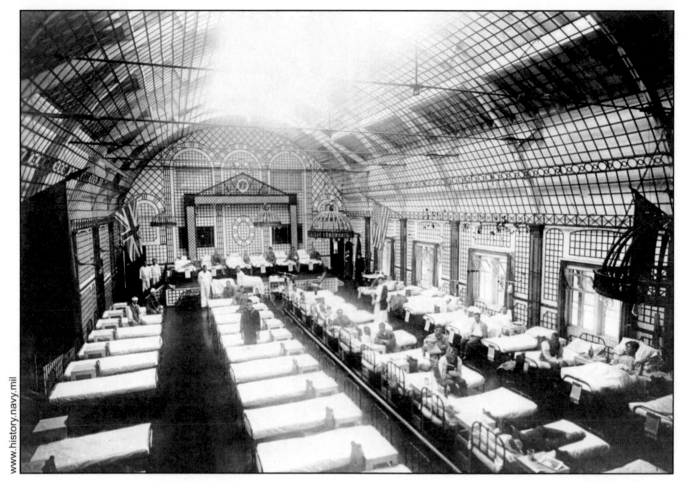

The Pavilion, which before the war had held concerts, was now fitted out with beds. There was also a wooden extension built at the rear, which can be seen in the photograph on page 61.

An ambulance unloading at Building No.3, the Pavilion.

The Lower Pump Room, now unfortunately destroyed, was an elegant glass-enclosed structure near the square and became a place for recovering patients to relax. The Countess of Cromartie also allowed use of the grounds and other facilities for tennis, croquet, football, and essential to Americans, baseball. Nearby buildings were also rented by the YMCA.[5]

Interior view of the pump room, used as a lounging room by convalescent patients from the hospital. Men sit on wicker chairs in a fancy lounge room decorated with ornate design and palm trees.

As with the bases, the US Navy organised their own facilities, bringing their own equipment and personnel. These are the officers based in Strathpeffer.

Hospital corpsmen, September 1918.

The hospital nursing staff, September 1918.

In a letter to Admiral William S Benson, Chief of Naval Operations, Admiral Henry T Mayo, Commander-in-Chief Atlantic Fleet wrote on 28 September 1918:

"Yesterday afternoon I went to the naval hospital at Strathpeffer, and Medical Inspector [Dr Edward S] Bogert and his assistant showed us all parts of his very large establishment. They have quite a number of patients at present, a large proportion being British. It certainly is a splendid hospital and, I understand, it is extremely popular, especially with the British, their patients stating, as gathered from censoring their letters, that they hoped they would be sent back there, rather than to a British hospital, in case it ever again became necessary for them to have hospital treatment."[6]

According to the Death Register of US Navy Base Hospital No.2, there were two accidental deaths of servicemen; one at each base and both in August 1918. In Invergordon a man was struck by a train and another drowned in the canal at Inverness. All illness-related deaths were recorded locally and the bodies returned to the United States as soon as possible on the ships returning home, after discharging their cargoes at Kyle of Lochalsh and Corpach.[7]

By April 1919 the hospital had been demobilised, bringing to a close the short-lived use of Strathpeffer by the US Navy.[8]

An unidentified couple from the Andrew Paterson studio.

An Amercian naval officer on a frozen lochan.

6. When the US Navy Came to Town
Inverness & Easter Ross

Wartime romance brings to mind films and novels. Many friendships, romances and eventually marriages were the result of the US presence in Inverness and Easter Ross. The sailors at both Base 17 and Base 18 and those serving on ships moored in the firths made their presence felt locally, as they paraded around streets and attended local dances.

The results led in some cases to local girls heading across the Atlantic Ocean to begin new lives in the USA once the war was over.

In a town the size of Inverness in 1919 it is very likely that many of the young women knew each other as over 80 women with Inverness connections married US sailors.

Sisters Catherine and Elizabeth Stuart both married in St Andrews Cathedral in Inverness within a year of each other and headed over the Atlantic in 1920 to join their respective US Navy husbands.

Catherine and Elizabeth Stuart.

One group of three friends all married US sailors. Ethel MacDonald and her close friend and neighbour Margaret Cowper met US Navy musicians, Ed Ramsay and Fred Peterson at a local dance where the men were playing in the band from their ship.

Ethel MacDonald and her family with American sailors. Ethel married Ed Ramsay.

The US Navy band that Ed Ramsay played in.

Another friend, Lena, a local children's nurse, met and married John Fowler, a Gunners Mate on the *USS San Francisco*. Family correspondence from much later noted: "Mindy tells me they were married over there. Ed came home (to US) on the Navy Ship, Ethel nine months later. Three Scottish girls met the Navy fellows at a dance and they all came here together."

The daughters of Inverness brothers, Andrew and James Paterson both married and left Inverness in the spring of 1919. They travelled on different ships and settled in different areas of America; Andrew's daughter Jessie in Pennsylvania while James's daughter Annie set up home many miles away in Kansas. For Jessie it was set to be a journey she would never forget. A warehouse checker, she married US sailor Percy Kemm in 1918. In March 1919 she, along with around 50 other war brides from various parts of the UK left the port of Liverpool on the *USS Louisville*, a liner converted to be used as a troop ship.

They headed to France to pick up US Military servicemen from their European bases before heading towards Ellis Island, New York.

One hundred miles out from the port of Brest in France, Louis (after the ship) Scott (after Scotland) Kemm was born by emergency Caesarean section, thankfully safely. He weighed in at over 8lbs. The entire crew and passengers held a collection for this special wee boy and this was given to Jessie when the ship docked in New York.

Jessie Paterson.

His birth certainly hit the headlines in America. Jessie and her new family set up home in Philadelphia, Pennsylvania and the couple went on to have another two children. Sadly Jessie was widowed just 10 years after arriving in the US and life was very hard for her with no family close by to turn to. Jessie never returned home to Inverness and passed away in Pennsylvania in November 1975, both her sons having served with US forces in the Second World War.

So far we only know a little about the lives of a handful of the women who left Inverness; a few did make the journey home on several occasions over the years to visit family and friends.

Annie Forbes, a local nurse, married Harry Peters in February 1919. He served as a Fireman on the *USS Black Hawk* which was moored close to Inverness. They did not have children and the couple travelled back to Inverness several times. Annie was widowed in the 1940s and moved to Seattle to be closer to her sister who had emigrated to Canada. While visiting her sister, Annie met and eventually married former Black Isle man, Duncan Cameron. The couple came back to Scotland to live in the 1950s, renting a farm close to Rosemarkie where they spent the rest of their lives.

Annie Paterson.

Though it is over 100 years since these women first made their way to new lives in the US there are family members here in Inverness who remember visits from the aunts and cousins over the years. Many still keep in touch with their overseas extended family. One lady remembers her mother's sister and family visiting Inverness on several occasions over the years and she herself took a trip out to Pennsylvania.

Annie Forbes.

Norman Finger.

Her aunt and her mother worked as transport drivers during the war — carrying goods from the rear of the Inverness Railway Station to the US Navy Bases in Inverness and Invergordon. They got to know many of the US sailors and remembered giving them lifts into Inverness hidden under the tarpaulin on the back of the carts.

Her aunt, Ina Bremner met and married Norman Finger and moved to the USA after the end of the war. Norman took many photographs during his time here and they have helped us to reveal the story of the US Navy in the Highlands.

Jeannie Russell.

Norman Finger took this photo on a ship's open day and it is thought Ina and Chrissie Bremner are amongst the group.

In June 1918 the marriage of local girl Jeannie Russell and US sailor Joseph M Hanzlik took place at the Roman Catholic Chapel in Inverness. This was one of the early marriages and the couple's daughter was born in Inverness as Jeannie waited to head to the US to join her husband.

In 2013 Joseph's grandson was the first member of his family to ever visit Inverness since the couple left.

A group of Norman Finger's shipmates in Inverness.

Through this contact we know that Joseph served as a Fireman on the *USS Swallow* and the images shared by the Hanzlik family illustrate the life of a US sailor during the First World War.

Deck crew of USS Swallow *heading to Alaska in 1920. Joseph Hanzlik was a crew member.*

Though we have touched on how hard it must have been for some of the wives to settle in the US, it must also have been quite a shock for some of the US sailors' parents, when they heard about their sons' marriages.

On 5 September 1919 Margaret Fraser Munro married Jesse Lattin at her home in Hill Terrace, Inverness.

An article appeared in the *Osage City Free Press* in Kansas on 2 October 1919 revealing that Mr and Mrs Lattin had just received a letter from their son Jesse, who was located at Base 18 in Scotland, to say he had married to a Miss Munro from Inverness. It went on to comment that Jesse was the first Osage City serviceman to "bring a young lady back from overseas."

Jesse (Aden) Lattin and Margaret Fraser Munro with her younger sister, Janet Fraser Munro, after the couple's wedding in Inverness on 5 September 1919.

Couples enjoying a walk through the Ness Islands.

A few local Invergordon girls married American sailors. The local girls were greatly charmed by the US Navy who had more money to spend than the British forces and local boys.[1] As all the sailors worked between Base 17 and Base 18, local girls met sailors from both bases. Many romances developed leading to some marriages and some births.

As the bigger town, many marriages took place in Inverness, although at least two marriages took place in Invergordon. Some romances were longstanding. In 1920 Isa Johnstone of Invergordon went to Guam to marry Dr Bartle who had been stationed at Dalmore.

The *Highland News* on 22 May 1920 reported:

"A wedding of local interest was solemnised on the 22nd March, in the Island of Guam, South Pacific, the contracting parties being Miss Isa D.R. Johnstone (Bunty), late of Broadford Cottage, Invergordon, and Dr William Gladstone Bartle, U.S. Navy (son of the late Rev. W.G. Bartle, of the same Service), who was recently stationed with the American Forces at Dalmore.

"The ceremony was performed at the residence of the Naval Chaplain, Captain Stone, and after the ceremony Captain Stone and Mrs Stone entertained the newly-married couple and the wedding guests, who numbered over forty. Handsome presents were received by Mr and Mrs Bartle from the inhabitants."

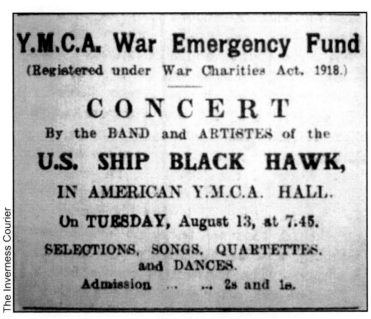

The Inverness Courier *12 August 1918.*

Westbrook, a friend of Wayne Abbott. He married a local girl, Elisabeth Fraser from Alness. She followed him back to the States.

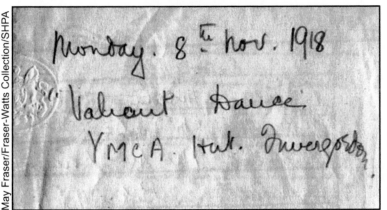

One of May Fraser's dance card programmes for the YMCA Hut at Invergordon, 8 November 1918, indicating Inverness lasses also attended events at the naval base there.

73

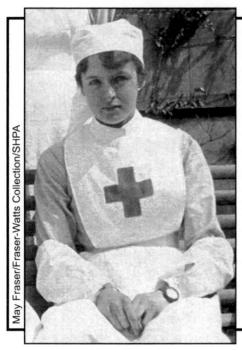

May Fraser, Voluntary Aid Detachment

Amateur photographer Mary Millicent 'May' Fraser (1898-1985) was the grand-daughter of Inverness ex-Provost Alexander Fraser (1880-1883). Her father, Lt.Col. Alexander Fraser, was an Inverness solicitor who had been killed at the Battle of Festubert in 1915.

May Fraser was a VAD nurse working at the Hedgefield House Red Cross Hospital in Inverness during the war. She and her sisters were part of the local social scene that entertained the American visitors at the many dances held in the town or at the Fraser property, Westwood, on Stratherrick Road.

Some 20 years after this photo was taken, she and her daughter would be two of the survivors of the sinking by U-boat of the 'SS Athenia' on 3 September 1939.

May Fraser.

May and her friends were invited to visit Base 18 and come aboard the ships of the US Navy.

Games of tennis were played on the court at Westwood.

Day outings included cycling around the countryside.

In the garden at Westwood, Stratherrick Road, in winter 1918.

A kettle was an important piece of kit when walking through the woods.

The Base 17 band, Invergordon.

Dances were held at Base 17, Dalmore and Base 18, Inverness as well as local halls. Each base had its own band as there were many accomplished musicians. The bands were in great demand in the Easter Ross and Inverness areas. Usually popular American music was played along with Scottish/English music. A song called 'The Force of Mine' was composed by HM Rubel and DM Yoder on board *USS Shawmut* and adopted as their squadron song.[2]

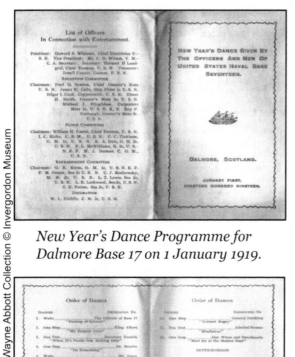

New Year's Dance Programme for Dalmore Base 17 on 1 January 1919.

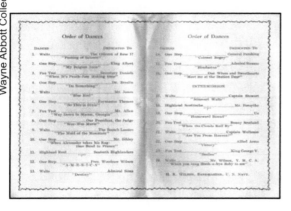

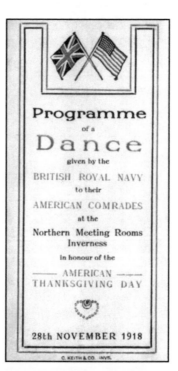

Dance card programme for the Northern Meeting Rooms in honour of Thanksgiving, 28 November 1918.

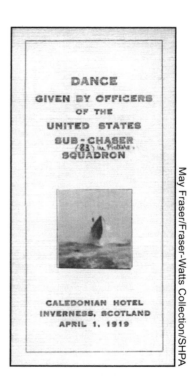

Dance card programme for the Caledonian Hotel given by the officers of the Sub-Chaser Squadron, 1 April 1919.

Andrew Paterson's wife Jean, and her daughter Constance both kept autograph books, as many of the great and good of the period would visit the Paterson home in Culduthel Road. Several of the entries are made by visiting officers from Base 18.

18 January 1919

When I met you.
While in the town of Invernes,
I walked along the River Ness.
Something there caught my eye,
'Twas a little lassie passing by.

She would not wait but strolled along,
Thinking she might get in wrong.
Down the lane and along the walk,
To another gob* she began to talk.

Now this little talk was enough to see,
That she would stand and talk to me.
So I went along and said Hello,
And as I did she began to go.

It was getting time to have some eats,
So I made sure that we would meet.
I said Hello in a gentle tone,
Then started towards the lassie's home.

But as time goes by, day by day,
I know what Connie will say.
The Black Hawk is the ship for me,
And I am sorry she went to sea.

But just as friends I must say as yet,
You are a lass I shall never forget.
And when we sail for far away,
I'll write to you from the U.S.A.

George J Fowler
U.S.S. Black Hawk
C/o G.P.O.
London Eng.
Home Address
329 Garden Street
Hoboken, N.J.
U.S.A.

*US military slang for sailor.

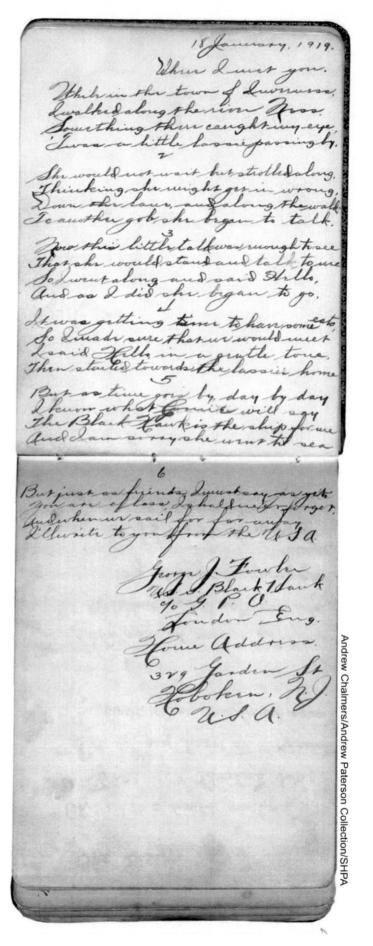

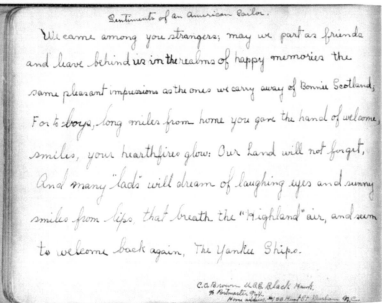

Kind Remembrances of a boy away from home who chewed gum and walked along High Street wearing white socks also a smile and said Dad Gumit "I'm an Amerikan" while often trying to "click" with a Scottish Lassie.

Wm. M. Johnson
U.S.S. Black Hawk
Jan. 16, 1919
Home address
135-8th St. Long Island City, N.Y.

Late Sunday afternoon on the Ness River

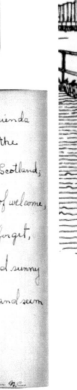

Sentiments of an American Sailor

We came among you strangers; may we part as friends and leave behind us in the realms of happy memories the same pleasant impressions as the ones we carry away from Bonnie Scotland; For to boys, long miles from home you gave the hand of welcome; smiles, your hearthfires glow: Our Land will not forget, and many "lads" will dream of laughing eyes and sunny smiles from lips, that breath the "Highland" air, and seem to welcome back again, The Yankee Ships.

C.O. Brown, U.S.S. Black Hawk
C/o Postmaster N.Y.
Home address, 12/36 Hunt St. Durham N.C.

In summer 2019, an autograph book was gifted to the Alness Heritage Centre from the family of Annabelle (Bella) Denoon, who had lived in Alness during the First World War. She collected many autographs of the sailors of the Mining Squadron at Dalmore.

Alness Heritage Centre

"Just for tonight only. What do you say Bella? DE Montgomery, Base 17 U.S.N. January 30 1918."

Annabelle (Bella) Denoon.

Alness Heritage Centre

Invergordon Museum

Postcard from a very hopeful young lady, posted on 2 April 1919. The message reads: "Hello Old Sport, how are you behaving since you went to Inverness. Flirting with all the nice girls I suppose. Hope to see you Wed so Cheerio till then. Joan."

Goodbye Base 17

It gaily fluttered in the breeze
The brave old Stars and Stripes
As we marched along the Alness shore
To the music of the pipes

To me it seemed but natural
And nothing out of place
This emblem dear to liberty
And all our Scottish race

And how that flag was planted there
Will live in song and story
With the coming of the Yanks to Dalmore
And their record of fresh Glory

How they crossed the seas in millions
Their bravest and their best
To fight with us for freedom
as we know were in the West

And how they acquit themselves like men
On sea and land in air
And won our favour and our hearts
By their valour everywhere

Now that their ever ending
Will keep their memory green
But we'll miss them and Old Glory
So Goodbye Base Seventeen.

— Annabelle Denoon 4 June 1919

However it was not all sweetness and love in Inverness. While the young women in Inverness were making new friends and meeting future husbands many men from Inverness were serving with UK forces all over Europe and beyond. In the months after hostilities ceased in November 1918 large groups of UK servicemen started to return home.

An altercation between a newly arrived batch of American sailors and local police who had asked them to 'move along' has led to much speculation as to the actual cause of a 'riot' on the streets of Inverness on the evening of 25 April 1919.

The conflict led to one local constable having his head badly smashed by the US Shore Patrol. There ensued a battle between US sailors, local civilians, local police and the Shore Patrol; it lasted over two hours and several arrests were made. It was widely reported in both local and national newspapers. One local lady recently recalled her father telling her, "The local boys chucked US servicemen who were heading back to their ships into the River Ness."

One particular tenement building in the Merkinch area off Grant Street — which came to be known locally as "Hill 60" — was well frequented by American sailors due to the friendliness of some of the female residents there.

The original "Hill 60" was a man-made hill in the Ypres battlefield area in Belgium, where the opposing armies continually captured, lost and then recaptured the position — so the Inverness "Hill 60" likely took its name from the continual change-over of military personnel too.

Victor Beals USNRF, The Northern Barrage 1919

A liberty party walking up Lower Kessock Street towards Grant Street and into Inverness.

Anon 1919 p32

Sporting events were very important as a morale booster and as team building exercises. The Yanks introduced the Highlands to the game of baseball. This was popular with the US personnel on the bases and ships as well as locals.[3] Having Telford Street Football Park (Caledonian FC) just across the road from Base 18 in Inverness was most convenient for sporting purposes, as shown in the photograph below.

A football game between 'Jackies' from Invergordon and Inverness, September 1918.

It wasn't long before many boys in the area were using a ball and a homemade bat to play the game, according to newspaper accounts in the States. Demonstration games were given at Bases 17 and 18. By the time the Squadron left, many Royal Navy ratings or locally based soldiers were practising hard in order to 'take on the Yanks' but the war ended and they left before an 'international' game could be played.[4]

Baseball team from the USS Shawmut.

Other inter-squadron sports included boat racing and wrestling. Track and field events used the Admiralty Recreation Grounds at Invergordon. Golf was also popular with the officers, and as well as the golf course next to Base 17, they would often sail down to Nigg Bay where the links was a favoured course.[5]

The American's sports equipment in Invergordon was kept in a store room next to the present Ship Inn. Most of the equipment was left when they went home but the store was not opened until after the Second World War by a local who lived in the building. An Aladdin's cave of sports gear was found including boxing gloves, archery equipment, baseballs and bats.[6]

One of the bats left behind in the sports equipment store.

Wayne Abbott, second from right, and friends on an old beached shipwreck at Invergordon in 1918.

The USS Housatonic.

7. The Ships of the Northern Barrage

A member of Admiral Sims' staff once wrote that the men who planted the North Sea mine barrage were, "living on the edge of eternity," for they went to sea in ships packed with high explosives.[1]

The makeshift minelayers included two former cruisers (relics of the 1880s), and eight converted merchantmen and passenger boats. In a fifty-hour period, they would steam out to position, form up three to five abreast at 500 yard intervals, drop overboard their one yard diameter mines containing 300 pounds of TNT, and return to base. "Precision and quickness of action while at sea were imperative, from start to finish," wrote Captain Belknap.[2]

Throughout the thirteen regular excursions, there could be no relaxation from tension. The actual discharging of the mines could last between just under four to seven hours, but cruising in darkness or in bad weather with such cargo kept everyone alert. As Belknap wrote his wife in August, "Interesting as these trips are, no sane person would take two for pleasure."[3]

Belknap was also appreciative of the excellent and friendly official and personal relations developed with the Royal Navy destroyer escort. The flotilla commander, Captain HR Godfrey CB DSO, wrote: "It was the determination of every officer and man in the 14th Flotilla, who had the honour of being entrusted with the screening of the US Minelaying Force, that no preventable attack by enemy submarine or surface vessel should inflict damage on any ship of the Force."[4]

Rear Admiral Clinton-Baker, head of the British minelaying force, called the Northern Barrage the "biggest mine planting stunt in the world's history."[5] On the following pages are the American ships that comprised Mine Squadron One and a series of photographs depicting the mine laying force in action.

The gathered fleet off Inverness from the shore.

May Fraser/Fraser-Watts Collection/SHPA

USS San Francisco, *flagship of Mine Squadron One under Captain HF Butler, joined the Allied effort of creating the North Sea mine barrage to restrict German U-boat traffic into the Atlantic.* San Francisco *laid a total of 9,102 mines.*[6]

USS Aroostook *was the Eastern Steamship Company's* Bunker Hill, *converted for mine planting under Captain JH Tomb.* Bunker Hill *and her sister ship* Massachusetts *were among the eight ships acquired by the US Navy in November 1917 and laid a total of 3,180 mines.*[7]

Anon 1919 p24

USS Baltimore *was converted to a mine layer with a capacity for 180 mines. On 2 June 1918 she joined Mine Squadron One under Captain AW Marshall at Inverness and for four months participated in laying 1,260 mines.*[8]

Anon 1919 p30

USS Black Hawk *moored off Inverness in September 1918 while serving as Mine Force repair ship and flagship. She was a destroyer tender launched in 1913 as* SS Santa Catalina *by William Cramp & Sons Ship and Engine Building Co., Philadelphia. She was purchased by the US Navy on 3 December 1917 and commissioned 15 May 1918 with Captain Roscoe C Bulmer in command. Note the dazzle camouflage pattern (called razzle dazzle in the US). She moved to Kirwall in Orkney for the North Sea mine sweep and remained there until 25 November 1919, still carrying out the duties of a repair and flagship. She was never involved in the actual minelaying or minesweeping.*[9]

Anon 1919 p34

USS Canandaigua, *the Southern Pacific freighter* El Sigio *converted for mine laying. Under Captain WH Reynolds from 7 June 1918 until 11 November 1918 she laid a total of 8,820 mines.*[10]

Anon 1919 p38

USS Canonicus, *originally the Southern Pacific Steamship Company freighter* El Cid *was commissioned on 2 March 1918 with Captain Thomas L Johnson in command. Canonicus cleared Newport, Rhode Island on 12 May 1918 and reached Inverness on 27 May 1918. Whilst operating as part of Mine Squadron One from 7 June 1918 until the close of the war, Canonicus planted 9,781 mines.*[11]

Anon 1919 p42

USS Housatonic *was the Southern Pacific freighter* El Rio, *temporarily converted for mine laying under Captain JW Greenslade. She planted 8,539 mines on the North Sea mine barrage.*[12]

Anon 1919 p50

USS Roanoke, *formerly the Southern Pacific freighter* El Dia, *under Captain CD Stearns she planted 8,236 mines.*[13]

Anon 1919 p60

USS Saranac, *was the Old Dominion Steamship Company* Hamilton *converted to enable her to carry mines on two decks. Saranac laid a total of 4,782 mines under Captain Sinclair Gannon. She then returned to the United States for decommissioning and returned to the steamship company in 1919.*[14]

Anon 1919 p66

USS Shawmut, *originally the passenger steamer* Massachusetts, *along with the* USS Aroostook, *headed for Scotland on 30 June 1918. The sea trials revealed that both ships consumed fuel at a higher rate than expected, raising concerns that they would be unable to make a non-stop Atlantic voyage. Commander Roscoe C Bulmer devised a plan to refuel both ships underway with hoses from the destroyer tender USS Black Hawk. Although this technique was uncommon at the time and was done during a gale, both ships successfully refuelled. Shawmut took part in ten mine laying excursions under Captain WT Cluverius, placing 2,970 mines for the North Sea mine barrage.*[15]

USS Quinnebaug *was the old Dominion Steamship Company Jefferson. The mine laying conversion enabled her to carry mines on two decks and included four Otis elevators individually capable of transferring two mines every 20 seconds from the storage deck to the launching deck. Under escort of British destroyers she completed ten mining missions under Commander D Pratt Mannix, planting approximately 6,040 mines in the North Sea mine barrage.*[16]

USS Patapsco *(Lieutenant WE Benson) and the* **USS Patuxent** *(Lieutenant JB Hupp) were two masted steel-hulled sea going tugs used for inspecting mine fields. Their main task was to experiment with ways to clear the mine fields after the armistice. Both were damaged clearing the mines, but were soon repaired and back in service.*[17]

The USS San Francisco *in dry dock at Invergordon.*

For transport, the mine rested on top of a 800lb steel anchor with wheels, allowing the mine assembly to be moved along a system of rails aboard the minelayer. The mine was attached to the anchor by a wire rope mooring cable stored on a reel.

Steam winches were used to haul trains or fleets of 20 to 40 mines each, aft to the feeding section. There the mines were seized by gangs of four men, who pushed each mine in turn up to the trap at the stern of the ship. Each time the trap was released a mine went overboard.[18]

Lighters filled with mines being towed by a mine carrier to the waiting ships.

Taking mines aboard. Hoisting mines out of the barge onto a minelayer.
The USS Arrowstook *is in the distance.*

Taking mines aboard the USS San Francisco.

Taking mines aboard the USS San Francisco.

Above the row of mines can be seen a marker buoy. This was used by the mine squadron to mark the end of a mine field when it was intended to resume that line on a subsequent expedition.

Allied naval officers on an inspection trip of the Northern Barrage, on board a US subchaser.

US minelayers at sea.

A minelayer laying a mine barrage protected by the guns of accompanying warships.

The US minelayers were escorted by British destroyers. Here a smoke screen is made by British destroyers to protect US Mine Laying Fleet. From left, USS Roanoke, USS Housatonic, USS Quinnebaug *and* USS Baltimore, *September 1918.*

Mine fleet manoeuvring in the North Sea, September 1918.

A 'premature'. There was a big concern with mines exploding once they were dropped over the side. Some 4,300 mines were calculated to have been lost to premature explosions.[19]

The Mine Force concert party which travelled to London to perform at the YMCA Eagle Hut on the Strand, WC on Wednesday 27 November 1918. This show included local girls from Inverness who danced and sang.

The Mining Squadron outside the main Dalmore Distillery building before departing for the United States, November 1918.

8. The End of the Bases

Operations continued until 26 October 1918 making a total of 13 mine laying trips. A further operation scheduled for the 30th was postponed, pending the Armistice. Before the Armistice was signed on 11 November 1918, the mine barrage was complete from Norway to within 10 miles of Orkney; the US Navy having assembled and laid in total 56,571 mines. However, after accounting for premature explosions this figure was reduced to 52,291 active mines in the minefield. Of these, 21,295 were accounted for in sweeping after the war — only 42.7 per cent of those that had been laid successfully![1]

The stores in the Inverness depot had a maximum storage capacity for 5,500 assembled units in addition to 5,000 mines and 5,000 sinkers with the corresponding small components. The maximum monthly output of the depot up to the Armistice had been 6,040 completed units.[2]

The total amount of mines supplied by Base 17 at Dalmore was 28,930 units with Base 18 at Inverness providing 27,641 mines.

The US Navy laid in total 57,470 mines (in addition to the units assembled in Scotland), with the British forces laying 13,546 mines in their sector. The grand total amount of mines forming the Northern Barrage was 70,117 units.[3]

The departure of the Mining Squadron from Base 17 at Invergordon was rapid. In December, and as no leave had been granted to officers and men since the beginning of hostilities, the Squadron were sent to Plymouth for a brief stay in order that all hands might have an opportunity to visit England before returning to the United States.

By 1 March 1919 Mine Force Base 17 was completely demobilized and turned over to the British Admiralty who replaced the American mines with their own.[4]

A fire in the ex-accommodation distillery stores however, delayed the handing back of the site to the distillery owners.[5] The Admiralty eventually handed back the distillery to Mackenzie Bros. in 1920, but production of whisky did not resume until 1923.[6] The warehouses and YMCA building were demolished between the wars.

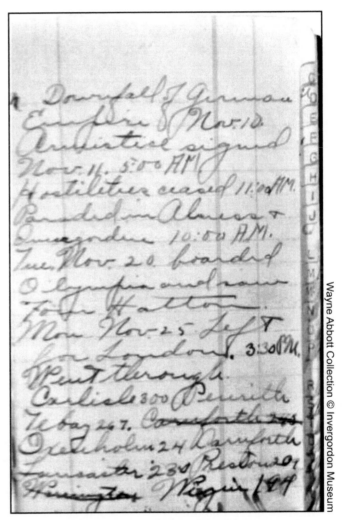

Wayne Abbott recorded the end of the war in his diary: "Downfall of German Empire Nov. 10. Armistice signed Nov. 11, 5:00AM. Hostilities ceased 11:00AM. Paraded in Alness & Invergordon 10:00AM. Tues. Nov. 20 boarded Olympia *and saw Tom Hatton. Mon. Nov. 25 left for London 3.30PM..."*

Anon 1919 p10

Letter dated 20 November 1918 from the Lord Lieutenant of Inverness-shire to Commander Belknap USN.

Because it was to be the primary base for mine sweeping operations Base 18 remained open after Base 17 closed down.[7] (It was eventually turned over to the Senior Naval Officer Inverness at 10 o'clock on 17 September 1919.)[8]

While waiting for delivery of the minesweepers and subchasers, the near 13,000 mines and 19,000 anchors were returned to the USA. There were also 2,500 men retained at the bases to man the 60 wooden fishing boats that were initially planned to use in the sweeping, but which would never be required.[9]

The riot in Inverness on 25 April (see page 83) between demobilized British soldiers and sailors and the American 'bluejackets', resulted in the suspension of 'liberty' for the rest of the time Base 18 remained open.[10]

On 1 October 1919, at the conclusion of the mine sweeping operations, the force started its phased return to the USA.[11]

Rear Admiral William S Sims USN
Supreme Commander US Naval Forces

Rear Admiral William Sowden Sims (1858-1936) was Supreme Commander of US Naval Forces operating in European Waters during the First World War. In February 1917 he was president of the Naval War College in Newport, Rhode Island. Just before the US entered the war Sims was posted to London as senior naval representative and in 1916 became the first captain of the battleship 'USS Nevada', the largest, most modern and most powerful ship in the US navy at that time. After the war Sims served a second tour as president of the Naval War College and it was during this time that he wrote and published his book 'The Victory at Sea' 'which described his experiences in the war. In 1921 the book won the Pulitzer Prize for History.

'The Victory at Sea' can be read online for free at the Project Gutenberg website: https://bit.ly/2W31GMX

www.history.navy.mil

The Supreme Commander of US Naval Forces in European Waters, Rear Admiral William S Sims wrote:

"These two mine-assembly bases at Inverness and Invergordon will ever remain a monumental tribute to the loyal and energetic devotion to duty of Captain Orin G Murfin, US Navy, who designed and built them; originally the bases were intended to handle 12,000 mines, but in reality Captain Murfin successfully handled as many as 20,000 at one time.

"It was here also that each secret firing device was assembled and installed, very largely by reserve personnel. As many as 1,200 mines were assembled in one day, which speaks very eloquently for the foresight with which Captain Murfin planned his bases."[12]

All that remained to do to complete the US involvement in the Northern Barrage was to launch a major sweeping operation to clear the North Sea of mines.

Captain Orin Gould Murfin.

USS Louisville *in New York Harbor while engaged in returning US service personnel from Europe in 1919. The Statue of Liberty is visible in the distance behind the stern.*

Mine laying crew of USS Utah *raising a mine that had been planted for practice.*

9. Taking up the Mines

Clearing the barrage after the war took 82 ships and five months working around the clock.[1] Taking up the mines proved to be far more hazardous than laying them. Mines had been planted at different depths but those designed to hinder surface shipping had antenna floating just eight to ten feet below the surface and contact with a piece of steel or iron no larger than a nail would be sufficient to operate the firing mechanism.[2]

The initial USN plan was to obtain around 60 'Scotch' wooden fishing boats and to encase their propellers in a wooden cage and to use them to sweep the surface mines with a wire sweep that would cause the mines to detonate. Then the more powerful steel hulled USN minesweepers would be free to sweep the deeper mines. Sweeping with two specially prepared wooden drifters had been tried in December 1918 and found to work.[3] These were Lowestoft fishing smacks – the *Red Fern* and *Red Rose* – which were hauled out at Inverness for preparation.[4] A severe storm and a close detonation turned this experiment into a drama.[5]

A minesweeper in action.

Daniels 1920b p10

Admiral Strauss was put in charge of the US sweeping.[6]

It was clear that the minelayers with their deep draughts could have no part in the sweeping operation and they sailed for the USA on 30 November 1918 but not before 400 trained petty officers and seamen had been taken off and transferred to the bases in case the fishing boats were needed.[7]

The *Black Hawk* remained in the Inverness Firth as the flagship together with tugs *Patapsco* and *Patuxent*.[8]

However, as this report below, believed to be written by Admiral Strauss states, a clever way had been proposed that would allow the USN steel-hulled sweepers to clear the surface mines:

"...Ensign Nichols, U.S.N.R.F., also of my staff, made a brilliant suggestion that promised to permit us to use our own steel minesweepers with their fine sea-going qualities and high power thereby making it unnecessary to borrow vessels from the British.

"Nichols' plan was to ground the positive pole of the electric generator to the hull well forward, and to carry the negative current to the sea well astern of the vessel in an insulated cable exposed only at its terminal. By this means a touch of the antenna on the steel hull instead of exploding the mine by the current generated by the contact, served to conduct a current to the mine which only held the armature more firmly in place.

"The scheme worked perfectly and it apparently only remained to sweep boldly through the field and blow up mines one after the other as the steel sweep-wire came in contact with the antenna wires, and at a safe distance astern of the sweepers."

Experiments were conducted using the *Patapsco* to see if the electric protection device worked and while it looked hopeful, the results were not conclusive.[9] However, a test sweep in the minefield indicated that some mines may have lost their antenna so would not detonate. These would need to be cut from their sinkers so they floated to the surface to be dealt with. Dealing with these was a task for subchasers and 20 of them were requested to be sent to Inverness by 1 April 1919.[10]

The subchasers started to arrive at Inverness in mid-February 1919 and 19 of them were in place by 1 March.[11] They practised sinking dummy mines and on 20 March, the tugs *Patuxent* and *Patapsco* with Captain Roscoe C Bulmer in command and fitted with a 'home made' electric protective device went to sea from Inverness for mine sweeping trials.

USN Subchaser 182 waiting to get through the top lock on the Caledonian Canal at Muirtown. Subchasers were small and fast naval vessels specifically intended for anti-submarine warfare, whereas minesweepers were small warships designed to engage in mine sweeping by using various mechanisms to counter the threat posed by naval mines.

Subchasers in the Caledonian Canal.

The trial was successful with 21 mines exploded and 17 cut adrift but a major risk was also highlighted which was that a chain reaction could be set off by an exploding mine ('counter-mining') and the 'chain' could be very close to the sweepers.[12]

On the return to Inverness from the trials, both Lerwick and Kirkwall were inspected as possible bases for sweeping as they were closer to the barrage. The new minesweepers were completed swiftly in US shipyards and the first 12 left Boston on 6 April for Inverness. By this time, it had been decided to use Kirkwall as the primary base but to retain Base 18 to receive supplies and provide a hospital facility.[13]

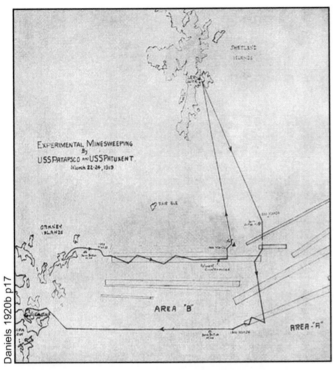

Chart showing the experimental sweeping by the USS Patapsco *and* USS Patuxent *22-24 March 1919.*

The first 12 sweepers arrived in the Inverness Firth on 20 April and hours later Admiral Strauss hoisted his flag on the *Black Hawk* and the flotilla departed on 29 April.[14]

The barrage area was marked out with light vessels and gas buoys by the British and joint sweeping operations took place between 29 April and 30 September 1919. Any mines adrift were detonated by rifle fire from US Navy subchasers, which followed on behind the sweepers.

This had been a very dangerous operation with several casualties and it is written that over half the mines were unaccounted for.

As recorded in *The Northern Barrage Taking up the Mines*:

"The *Patuxent* was the first victim. On May 12 the sweep had been severed by an explosion and had to be hauled on board to be repaired. When the kite was within sight a mine could be seen hanging by its mooring cable.

"The commanding officer immediately sent all hands forward to a place of safety, going aft himself to clear it with the assistance of his chief boatswain's mate. The mine was on the surface about 10 feet from the side of the ship when suddenly, without apparent cause, it exploded. Several men were blown overboard by the mass of flying water, but all were rescued.

"The commanding officer, who at the time of the explosion was only a few feet from the mine, escaped with the loss of his thumb, which was amputated by a flying fragment. Since the force of the explosion had been largely spent in the air, the damage to the ship was not serious, and a few days in dry dock were sufficient to repair her."[15] There was significant loss of life and loss of some vessels with many more damaged.[16]

At the end of 1919, sweeping for moored buoyant mines was suspended for the winter. There had been losses to civilian ships; in October 1919 20 crewmen drowned when the Swedish steamship *Hollander* sank minutes after striking a mine and in December the steamer *Kerwood* struck a mine and sank.[17] The following spring the Royal Navy resumed minesweeping operations to clear sunken mines from fishing grounds and searching for mines that had broken free and gone adrift.

Sinking a mine by rifle fire.

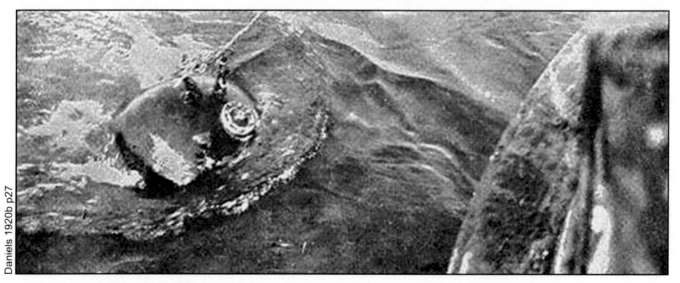

A mine foul of the USS Patuxent's *kite. The mine exploded in less than a minute after this picture was taken.*

Of 54 new US minesweepers built in the First World War, 34 were employed on the Northern Barrage.[17] One of them, the USS Pelican, was completely disabled by a mine explosion.

A mine is exploded on contact with an electrically charged sweeping cable during the operation to clear the minefield after hostilities ended.

A complete un-exploded Mark VI mine recovered during the operations from sweeping the Northern Barrage in May 1919. TNT is lying on the deck and this mine exploded shortly after the photograph was taken.

Retrieved mine shells in an undisclosed location.

ERRATA

Page 125, after paragraph 2 add: The following submarines were sunk in the Northern Mine Barrage:

Area	Submarine	Date
B	U-92	September 9, 1918
B	U-102	September -- (Probable)
A	U-156	September 25, 1918
B	UB-104	September 19, 1913
B	UB-127	September -- (Probable)
A	UB-123	October 19, 1918

Sources: The Submarine Warfare by Micholson and British Submarine Losses Return 1919.

The amended figures in the 1920 book, The Northern Barrage and Other Mining Activities *by Secretary of the US Navy Josephus Daniels, indicated the claimed success rate was four U-boats sunk and two probable.*

10. Success Rate and Consequences

So how successful was the Northern Barrage? In his 1920 book, Josephus Daniels stated: "It is well to remember that a mine barrage of this nature can never be an absolute barrier possessing 100 per cent efficiency. On account of the necessity of laying the mines at a distance of approximately 300 feet apart in order to reduce the possibility of counter-mining, it would always be possible for a submarine with a beam of approximately 30 feet to successfully cross such a barrier no matter how many parallel lines of mines may be laid. The danger in crossing, of course, increases with the number of rows of mines but not in direct proportion. The object, then, in constructing a barrage must be to make the danger incurred by the passage of a vessel sufficiently great to prevent submarines from taking the risk involved."[1]

The design of the minefield meant there was a theoretical 66 percent chance of a surfaced U-boat triggering a mine and a 33 percent chance for a submerged U-boat.[2] As the last mines were laid only a matter of days before the end of the war, it is impossible to assess the overall success of the plan. Some believe the minefield was a major cause of the declining morale of the Imperial German Navy through the final months of the war, while others suggest Germany easily swept safe channels through the large, unguarded minefield.[3]

Daniels wrote: "With the information at present available, it appears that a total of six submarines were destroyed in the barrage and possibly an equal number were severely damaged. On account of the difficulty of obtaining accurate information, such a short time after the Armistice was signed, it is highly probable that subsequent data will show even greater damage to have been done."[4]

9 September 1918 — U-92

A type U87 submarine built in the Kaiserliche Werft shipyard in Danzig and launched on 12 May 1917. Her first commander was Kapitänleutnant Max Bieler. On 1 June 1918 he passed command to Kapitänleutnant Günther Ehrlich (1886-1918). The U-92 was credited with five ships sunk with a total of 15,961 tons and two ships damaged with a total of 7,373 tons. On 9 September 1918 she was mined in the Northern Barrage east of the Orkney Islands with all 42 hands lost. The wreck of U-92 was located by a sonar sweep in 2006 and information to confirm the identification was obtained by divers in 2007.[5]

Günther Ehrlich.

25 September 1918 — U-156

A type U151 submarine built in the Atlas Werke shipyard in Bremen and launched on 17 April 1917. Her first commander was Kapitänleutnant Konrad Gansser. On 16 June 1918 he passed command to Kapitänleutnant Richard Feldt (1882-1918). The UB-156 was credited with 44 ships sunk with a total of 50,471 tons, two ships damaged with a total of 638 tons, and one warship sunk, the *USS San Diego* 10 miles off Fire Island, New York. It was one of the largest ships hit with a total 13,680 tons. On 25 September 1918 the UB-156 was probably mined in the Northern Barrage with all 77 hands lost, as she failed to report when clear.[6]

Richard Feldt.

Anon 1919 p110

Writing in 2018, Dennis Conrad in an essay on the Navy History and Heritage Command website asked the question if the barrage had been effective and worth the cost. Secretary of the Navy Josephus Daniels was confident that it was and believed not laying the barrage earlier had been the greatest naval error of the war.

Conrad wrote "Historians are not so sure. The best estimate is that six German submarines were destroyed and that it affected the morale and efficiency of the German submarine service. However, other historians have argued that the resources spent on the barrage would have been more profitably used elsewhere.

"In the end, the question can never be determined definitively because the barrage was still unfinished when the war ended; the Norwegians had not yet mined their territorial waters, leaving the Germans a path through the minefield to open sea."[7]

Research during the last 100 years has resulted in an almost exact accounting for the U-boats lost to the Northern Barrage. The website www.uboat.net records the fate of all German submarines during both world wars. (The other U-boat listed by Daniels in his 1920 book as a casualty of the Northern Barrage, the UB-104 under Oberleutnant Thomas Bieber, is now recorded as disappearing on 21 September 1918 in Lyme Bay for an unknown reason with all 36 hands lost.)

www.uboat.net

Curt Beitzen.

29 September 1918 — U-102

A type U57 submarine built in the AG Weser shipyard in Bremen and launched on 12 May 1917. Her first commander was Kapitänleutnant Ernst Killman. On 26 November 1917 he passed command to Kapitänleutnant Curt Beitzen (1885-1918). The U-102 was credited with 12 ships sunk with a total of 16,746 tons and two ships damaged with a total of 3,744 tons. She is also credited with sinking one warship (10,850 tons) and one ship taken as a prize (1,700 tons). Between 28 and 30 September 1918 she was homebound and was mined east of the Orkney Islands with all 42 hands lost. The wreck of U-102 was located by a sonar sweep in 2006 and information to confirm the identification was obtained by divers in 2007.[8]

While serving as commanding officer of U-75 on 29 May 1916 Beitzen had laid a 38-piece minefield with U-75 just outside the entrance to Scapa Flow. That same day the *HMS Hampshire* left Scapa for Russia. On board was Field Marshal Lord Kitchener and his general staff. Only 10 miles outside Scapa Flow the armoured cruiser ran onto one of Beitzen's mines in foul weather. She sank in minutes, leaving only 14 survivors, and Great Britain's most famous military leader was one of the casualties.[9]

30 September 1918 — UB-127

A type UBIII submarine built in the AG Weser shipyard in Bremen and launched on 27 April 1918. Her commander was Oberleutnant Walter Scheffler (1880-1918). Although he had sunk six ships with the UB-21, the UB-127 had no successes, and in fact had only been 10 days into its first patrol when she was possibly mined south of Fair Isle passage sometime after 9 September with the loss of 34 hands.[10]

Walter Scheffler.

Robert Ramm.

19 October 1918 — UB-123

A type UBIII submarine built in the AG Weser shipyard in Bremen and launched on 2 March 1918. Her first commander was Kapitänleutnant Max Bieler. On 1 June 1918 he passed command to Oberleutnant zur See Robert Ramm (1890-1918). The UB-123 was credited with one ship sunk, the *RMS Leinster* with a total of 2,646 tons and one ship damaged with a total of 4,095 tons. Three ships were taken as a prize (total 3,530 tons). On 19 October 1918 she was mined in the Northern Barrage with all 36 hands lost.[11]

The barrier of high explosive across the North Sea; 10,000 tons of TNT spread over an area 230 miles long by 25 miles wide and reaching from near the surface to 240 feet below; 70,000 anchored mines each containing 300 pounds of explosive, sensitive to a touch, barring the passage of German submarines between Orkney and Norway — this was the final five months' contribution of the American and British mining forces towards bringing the war to a close.

Besides influencing an early armistice, this great minelaying operation marked an epoch in the use of submarine mines in warfare.

Although its tactical effectiveness is debatable, the Northern Barrage had a profound impact on the Highlands, and in a speech by Admiral WS Sims to the men of the Force on board *USS San Francisco* at Portland, England on 12 December 1918, he recognised one lasting effect the American bases had on the area.

"That good feeling you have been able to show has made this nation understand the Americans now the way they never did before, and you people understand the English and Scotch people as you never did before. It makes good feeling on both sides of the ocean, and to keep the peace of the world we are going to need that feeling among all the Anglo-Saxons."

The U-boats Are Out! *The famous German film poster of 1917 by Hans Rudi Erdt.*

Notes

1 Introduction

1   www.uboat.net/wwi/boats
2   www.history.navy.mil
3   Belknap (1920) p110
4   Daniels (1920a) p13
5   USN General Board document G.B.No.425-5 dated 24 October 1917
6   Daniels (1920a) p71
7   Daniels (1920a) p59
8   Taylor (1965) Ch 2 states after Jutland "...their High Seas fleet only left harbour again three times in the course of the war, and then to no purpose."
9   www.uboat.net/wwi/boats
10 Terraine (2009) p766
11 Borer (1970) Ch 5
12 www.fold3.com/image/296968041 for full report and onwards.
13 Orin Gould Murfin went on to become a four-star admiral and Commander-in-Chief of the Asiatic Fleet.
14 Daniels (1920a) p63
15 Daniels (1920a) p64
16 Daniels (1920a) p64
17 Belknap (1920) p23
18 Belknap (1920) p23
19 Belknap (1920) p48
20 Daniels (1920a) p90
21 Daniels (1920a) p120
22 Daniels (1920a) p120
23 Daniels (1920a) p67

2 US Navy Base 18 Inverness

1   Ash (1991)
2   Anon (1920)
3   Highland Archives – Merkinch School Log Book
4   Aberdeen Press & Journal 16 May 1919
5   Anon (1920)
6   Anon (1920)
7   Anon (1920)
8   Anon (1920)
9   Anon (1920)
10 Anon (1920)
11 Hartmann (1975) pp16-17
12 Anon (1920)
13 Anon (1920)
14 Anon (1920)
15 Paterson's Inverness Portraits, www.patersoncollection.co.uk

3 US Navy Base 17 Dalmore

1   Daniels (1920a) p66
2   Daniels (1920a) p85 & p104; Belknap (1920) pp12-13
3   Daniels (1920a) p65
4   Anon (1920) p5
5   Pratt (1921) p542
6   Anon (1920) p5
7   Anon (1920) p6
8   Pratt (1921) pp539-541
9   Pratt (1921) p947
10 Pratt (1921) p541
11 Baxter & Campbell (2020) pp28-31
12 Ash (1991)
13 Crompton (2020) pp6-7
14 Anon (1920) p6
15 Highland News 13 September 1924

Victor Beals USNRF, The Northern Barrage 1919

4 Defending Base 18

1 www.fold3.com
2 www.fold3.com
3 National Archives ADM 116/1570
4 National Archives ADM 116/1570. Highland Archives: Fortrose Town Council Minutes 29.07.1918; Black Isle District Committee Minutes 10.06.1918; Black Isle Poorhouse accounts.
5 *The Inverness Courier* 1918
6 Highland Archive Centre
7 *Daily Record*, 1916 — Real War Work by Women
8 Reid (2001) p147
9 www.clydeships.co.uk

5 US Navy Hospital in Strathpeffer

1 *Annual Report of the Surgeon General* pp81-82
2 Different sources provide different totals. A letter from Vice Admiral Sims to his wife 1 June 1918 stated 500 (www.history.navy.mil). The *Annual Report of the Surgeon General*, US Navy for 1919 stated 600, and a Navy publication on the Northern Barrage published in 1920 said 1,000 (Belknap, p23).
3 *Annual Report of the Surgeon General* p197
4 Pratt (1921) p566; Anon (1920) p5
5 *Annual Report of the Surgeon General* pp81-82
6 www.history.navy.mil archive TL, DLC-MSS, Mayo Papers, Box 10.
7 Department of the Navy. Bureau of Medicine and Surgery. Burial Records, compiled 1898-1931. ARC ID: 2694772. Records of the Bureau of Medicine and Surgery, 1812-1975, Record Group 52 available through Ancestry.com
8 Letter from Rear Admiral Henry S Knapp, Commander, United States Naval Forces Operating in European Waters, to Secretary of the Navy Josephus Daniels and Admiral William S Benson, Chief of Naval Operations. (www.history.navy.mil)

6 When the US Navy Came to Town

1 Daniels (1920a) pp21-22
2 Anon (1919) pp93-95
3 Anon (1919) p88
4 Belknap (1920) p50
5 Anon (1919) pp88-89
6 Duncan MacLeod who owns one of the bats, played with the boxing gloves and other equipment when a child. It was his father who opened the store.

7 The Ships of the Northern Barrage

1 www.worldwar1.com/dbc/nsminebr.htm
2 Coffman (2014)
3 Coffman (2014)
4 Belknap (1920) p6
5 Belknap (1920) p5
6 Daniels (1920a); www.history.navy.mil; Wikipedia passim.
7 Daniels (1920a); www.history.navy.mil; Wikipedia passim.
8 Daniels (1920a); www.history.navy.mil; Wikipedia passim.
9 Daniels (1920a); www.history.navy.mil; Wikipedia passim.
10 Daniels (1920a); www.history.navy.mil; Wikipedia passim.
11 Daniels (1920a); www.history.navy.mil; Wikipedia passim.
12 Daniels (1920a); www.history.navy.mil; Wikipedia passim.
13 Daniels (1920a); www.history.navy.mil; Wikipedia passim.
14 Daniels (1920a); www.history.navy.mil; Wikipedia passim.
15 Daniels (1920a); www.history.navy.mil; Wikipedia passim.
16 Daniels (1920a); www.history.navy.mil; Wikipedia passim.
17 Daniels (1920a); www.history.navy.mil; Wikipedia passim.
18 www.history.navy.mil - NH 123953 A fleet of mines, North Sea
19 Daniels (1920a) p67

8 The End of the Bases

1 Daniels (1920a) p67
2 Anon (1920) *Minelaying Bases at Grangemouth, Dalmore & Glen Albyn*
3 Belknap (1920) p110
4 Daniels (1920a) pp10 & 17
5 *Highland News* 29 March 1919 & *Ross-shire Journal* 28 March 1919
6 Records of Mackenzie Bros., Dalmore Ltd
7 Daniels (1920b) p17
8 Daniels (1920) p69
9 Daniels (1920b) p13
10 Daniels (1920b) p22
11 Daniels (1920a) p69
12 Sims (1920) Project Gutenberg website

9 Taking up the Mines

1 Gilbert (2001) p4
2 Daniels (1920b) p8
3 Report presumed to be written by Admiral Strauss, www.fold3.com
4 Daniels (1920b) p11
5 Daniels (1920b) pp14-15
6 Daniels (1920b) p9
7 Daniels (1920b) p9
8 Daniels (1920b) pp9-10
9 Daniels (1920b) pp15-16
10 Daniels (1920b) p16
11 Daniels (1920b) p16
12 Daniels (1920b) p18
13 Daniels (1920b) p19
14 Daniels (1920b) p22
15 Daniels (1920b) p27
16 Daniels (1920b) passim. One vessel, the *Richard Bulkeley*, was sunk by the explosion of a fouled mine and many others were either permanently disabled or so damaged that dry docking was necessary. There were 10 fatalities all told; one man was crushed on deck by machinery, and nine men, including two commanding officers, were killed or drowned as a result of exploding mines.
17 www.wartimememoriesproject.com

10 Success Rate and Consequences

1 Daniels (1920a) p125
2 Daniels (1920a) p125
3 Potter (1960) p470
4 Daniels (1920a) p125
5 www.uboat.net
6 www.uboat.net
7 www.history.navy.mil
8 www.uboat.net
9 www.uboat.net
10 www.uboat.net
11 www.uboat.net

Further Information

More information on the local projects covering Base 18 Inverness, Base 17 Dalmore and the Northern Barrage, can be found online.

Inverness Local History Forum
www.invernesshistory.co.uk website for a selection of images of Base 18 Inverness.

Invergordon Museum
www.invergordonmuseum.co.uk website for information on both the 'Wartime Dalmore' and 'Invergordon in World War I' projects.

Groam House Museum
www.groamhouse.org website for information on the 'Rosemarkie, Fortrose and Avoch in World War I Project'.

Petty and Ardersier Community Heritage
www.facebook.com/oldPettyandArdersier for regular updates of local historical interest.

Archaeology for Communities in the Highlands
www.archhighland.org.uk/arch-projects.asp for ARCH projects on 'Remembering the Strathpeffer Area', 'Invergordon in World War I', and 'Wartime Dalmore'.

Bibliography

Annual Report of the Surgeon General. US Navy for the Fiscal Year 1919

ANON. (1919) *The Northern Barrage, Mine Force, United States Atlantic Fleet, the North Sea 1918.* US Naval Institute, Annapolis

ANON. (1920) *Minelaying Bases at Grangemouth, Dalmore & Glen Albyn.* Admiralty Technical History & Index Vol.6 Part 45

ASH, Marinell (1991) *This Noble Harbour: A History of the Cromarty Firth.* Cromarty Firth Port Authority, Invergordon

BAXTER, RT & CAMPBELL, JDS (2020) *WWI Dalmore Branch,* Far North Express Issue 80 (May 2020)

BELKNAP, Reginald Rowan (1920) *The Yankee Mining Squadron or Laying the North Sea Mine Barrage.* US Naval Institute, Annapolis

BORER, Mary Cathcart (1970) *The First World War.* Macmillan, London

CHURCHILL, Winston S (1938) *The World Crisis 1911-1919.* Vol.2 Odhams Press, London

COFFMAN, Edward M (2014) *The War to End All Wars: The American Military Experience in World War I.* University Press of Kentucky

CROMPTON, Nigel (2020) *Dalmore Distillery's Fire Heritage,* Fire Cover Issue 229 (August 2020)

DANIELS, Josephus (1920a) *The Northern Barrage and Other Mining Activities.* US Office of Naval Records & Library, Publication No.2, Government Printing Office, Washington

DANIELS, Josephus (1920b) *The Northern Barrage (Taking up the Mines).* US Office of Naval Records & Library, Publication No.4, Government Printing Office, Washington

DUFEIL, Yves (2011) *Kaiserliche Marine U-Boote 1914-1918.* Histomar Publications, online title, www.uboat.net

GILBERT, Jason A (2001) *Combined Mine Countermeasures Force,* Newport, Rhode Island

HARTMANN, Gregory K (1975) *Mine Warfare History & Technology,* Naval Service Weapons Center, Maryland

LECANE, Philip (2005) *Torpedoed! The RMS Leinster Disaster.* Periscope Publishing Ltd, Reading

POTTER, EB & NIMITZ, Chester (1960) *Sea Power,* Prentice-Hall, New Jersey

PRATT, Edwin A (1921) *British Railways and the Great War. Organisation, efforts, difficulties and achievements.* Selwyn & Blount Ltd, London

REID, J (2001) *Steam Drifters Recalled: Whitehills to St. Combs,* J&M Reid, Moray

SIMS, William S (1920) *The Victory at Sea.* Doubleday, Page & Co, Garden City

TAYLOR, AJP (1965) *English History 1914-1945.* Clarendon Press, Oxford

TERRAINE, John (2009) *Business in Great Waters: U-boat Wars 1916-1945.* Pen & Sword Military, Barnsley

Organisations

Alness Heritage Centre
Groam House Museum, Rosemarkie
Highland Archive Centre, Inverness
Historic Environment Scotland, Edinburgh
Imperial War Museum, London
Invergordon Museum
Inverness Local History Forum, Inverness
Maxar Technologies
National Library of Scotland, Edinburgh
National WWI Museum & Memorial, Kansas City, MO, USA
Petty & Ardersier Community Heritage
Scottish Highlander Photo Archive (SHPA), Inverness
The National Archives, Kew

Websites

www.clydeships.co.uk
www.history.navy.mil
(Naval History & Heritage Command)
www.invernesshistory.co.uk
www.patersoncollection.co.uk
www.subchaser.org
www.uboat.net
www.wartimememoriesproject.com
www.worldwar1.com

Newspapers

Aberdeen Press & Journal
Daily Record
Highland News
The Inverness Courier

Acknowledgements

In 1919 the US Navy packed its bags and left the Highlands of Scotland after a stay of almost two years, in which time its presence saw one of the most ambitious and largest maritime operations ever undertaken. This almost forgotten era in local history was largely unknown until recently.

Not so now though, as local history groups have conducted much research and location searches to identify what remains of the presence of the American Navy. This information was collected and presented in most interesting form by several groups — Inverness Local History Forum, Alness Heritage Centre, Invergordon Museum, Groam House Museum (Rosemarkie) and Petty & Ardersier Community Heritage SCIO — who came together with Highlife Highland, Historic Environment Scotland, and Archaeology for Communities in the Highlands (ARCH) to present a comprehensive one-day Conference on The Northern Barrage in October 2019.

It would have taken much more than one full day to recount ALL of the history and stories which have been so far uncovered, so the Conference could do no more than give a flavour of the effect of the American presence in the area, and all those who attended went away with far more information than previously.

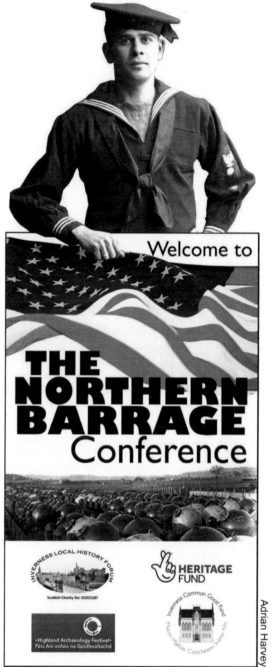

Inverness Local History Forum wish to express a sincere gratitude to all those who contributed to the Conference by speaking on their local 'specialist subject' and who staged excellent exhibitions of photographs and plans, all of which were greatly appreciated by those who attended the Conference, Exhibition and Evening Talk.

Particular thanks are due to the National Lottery Heritage Fund and Inverness Common Good Fund for their financial support, Inverness Deputy Provost Graham Ross for officially opening the conference, Allan Kilpatrick (HES) for his co-chairing the event and providing such a thought-provoking and informative evening talk, Dr Susan Kruse MBE of ARCH for her chairing and being a prime-mover in the arranging and organisation of the event, Maureen T Kenyon (ILHF President), Dave Conner (ILHF Convenor), Allan Cameron (ILHF Vice President), Adrian Harvey (ILHF Vice-convenor/Publications Editor), Anne C MacKintosh (ILHF Researcher), and all the other ILHF Committee and members for all their hard work in organising the successful event. It is out of that Conference that the present volume was created.

This book was written by members of the Inverness Local History Forum, Alness Heritage Centre, Invergordon Museum, participants from the Groam House Museum Rosemarkie, Fortrose and Avoch in WWI Project, and ARCH in a prime example of collaboration.

Allan Kilpatrick of HES presents his evening talk to guests at The Northern Barrage Conference held in Inverness, 3 October 2019.

Contributing writers include Dave Conner, Maureen T Kenyon, Allan Cameron, Anne C MacKintosh, Adrian Harvey, Susan Kruse, Bob Baxter, Alasdair Cameron, Stewart Campbell, Valerie Campbell-Smith, Catherine Gaston, Alan Kinghorn, Duncan MacLeod, Una McIntosh, Jacky Roberts, Carolyn Samsin, Malcolm Standring, Ron Stewart, Ivan Brazier, Barbara Cohen, Don Holding, Richard Jenner, Janet Witheridge and Robin Witheridge.

We thank the following organisations for permission to reproduce images: Naval History and Heritage Command, Imperial War Museum, Scottish Highlander Photo Archive, Invergordon Museum, Alness Heritage Centre, The National Archives, National Library of Scotland, National WWI Museum and Memorial USA, Maxar Technologies, www.uboat.net, and Todd A Woofenden (www.subchasers.org).

We must also thank contributors who have gifted contemporary personal memorabilia to the various organisations: Andrew Chalmers for the Andrew Paterson Collection, Heather Watts for the May Fraser Collection, John Bowen for the Wayne Abbott Collection, the late Robert Paterson for the Robert Paterson Collection, Eileen Kemm Morton, Kemm Family Archive, Joseph M Hanzlik, Papa's Postcards Collection and Hanzlik Family Archive, Jesse (Aden) Lattin Family Archive, Eileen Cunningham, Roseann Christie, Duncan MacLeod, John MacLaren and Norman Stewart.

Also thanks to our own Inverness Local History Forum members: Mrs C Reid, Mrs Alison Dougherty and Mrs Joy Crosiar for allowing us to use their photograph collections, letters and family history information; the Forum Northern Barrage steering committee, Dave Conner, Maureen T Kenyon, Allan Cameron, Anne C MacKintosh, Mary MacRae, Adrian Harvey; and thanks to teclan Ltd for the use of their production facilities.

Scottish Charity No: SC025287

The Inverness Local History Forum was founded in 1992 by the late Mrs Sheila Mackay OBE. With a few like-minded volunteers she set about researching, recording, preserving and promoting the history of Inverness.

The long-term objective of the project was to record all aspects of social life in what was then the Burgh of Inverness. The Forum has to date archived over 200 hours of oral history recordings by local people, collected books, photographs, maps and other artefacts of interest relating to our history. The Forum has also published several popular books and booklets, as well as *Inverness Remembered*, a quarterly newsletter for members which has surpassed 90 issues since its inception last century.

The Forum presents regular talks and presentations from guest speakers throughout the year on a variety of topics, held on the first Wednesday of every month at 2.00pm (except January, July, August and December). These talks, of just under one hour duration, are held in the theatre of the Spectrum Centre in Margaret Street, Inverness, alongside the bus station.

The Forum has a website at **www.invernesshistory.co.uk** and also maintains a presence on Facebook (**www.facebook.com/InvernessLocalHistory**) — where an ever-growing series of illustrated historical articles about people, places, links to websites of interest and current events can be found.

The organisation is a registered charity and all profits from the sale of this book will be used to continue the Forum's work in unearthing the hidden nuggets of information and memorabilia that get lost or forgotten in this fast-paced modern world and the mists of time.

invernesslocalhistoryforum@gmail.com

Inverness Local History Forum is registered as a Scottish Charity: SC025287